W9-BJR-945

POLAND

TITLES IN THE MODERN NATIONS OF THE WORLD SERIES INCLUDE:

Brazil
Canada
China
Cuba
Egypt
England
Germany
Greece
India
Ireland
Italy
Japan
Kenya
Mexico
Norway
Poland
Russia
Somalia
South Africa
South Korea
Spain
Sweden
The United States
Vietnam

POLAND

BY LAUREL CORONA

Poland /
943.8 COR

LUCENT BOOKS
P.O. BOX 289011
SAN DIEGO, CA 92198-9011

Library of Congress Cataloging-in-Publication Data

Corona, Laurel, 1949–
    Poland / by Laurel Corona.
        p.   cm. — (Modern nations of the world)
Includes bibliographical references and index.
Summary: A discussion of Poland including its history, struggle for
sovereignty, Nazi and Communist rule, cultural heritage, and modern
day life.
    ISBN 1-56006-600-8
    1. Poland—Juvenile literature.   [1. Poland.]   I. Title.   II. Series.
    DK4147 .C67   2000
    943.8—dc21

                                                                    99-050797

CONTENTS

INTRODUCTION

POLAND—PROUD AND FREE

"Poor Poland! They go on sadly there."[1] These words, written by English poet Samuel Taylor Coleridge in 1794, echo a common view of Poland as one of history's victims. Though gray images of Nazi invasion and communist oppression are the first things that spring to many people's minds when they think of Poland, its past and present are far more diverse than those few images would suggest.

POLAND'S RISE AND FALL

For several centuries during the first millennium, the Poles were anything but victims of those around them. By around A.D. 500, the Polanie, a collection of Slavic peoples, lived in small settlements on the southern reaches of a great plain which sweeps without interruption across most of northern Europe. The nation of Poland, named for the Polanie, was founded by a count named Mieszko in A.D. 966 as a way to keep the Polanie from becoming victims of the nations around them. For several centuries after Mieszko, shrewd Polish rulers were able not only to defend Poland against all but the most fleeting of occupations of small parts of its territory, but to expand Poland into an empire stretching north along the Baltic into today's Russian Federation and Lithuania, and east into today's Ukraine and Belarus. For substantial stretches of time between 1000 and 1600, Poland was the major power in eastern Europe.

The history of those centuries is a source of pride for the Poles and an important part of their national identity. However, in the centuries that followed, Poland's power waned, and the nation shrank and splintered. By 1800 Poland could not even be found on current maps, having been divided up by Austria, Prussia, and Russia, and made part of their empires. The century that followed what are called the Partitions of Poland was a time of great introspection for the Poles. Told by their occupiers that they would from then on call themselves Prussian (German), Austrian, or Russian, and be considered citizens of those empires, the Poles refused to submit to the loss of their culture and nation. Many paid with their lives in political uprisings, and others found that to express themselves proudly as Poles they had to leave their beloved country and live as immigrants elsewhere. It was in the nineteenth century, when their land was not their own, that Poles understood that Poland is as much a state of mind, an idea, as it is a place.

A Timeless and Contemporary Land

It is, however, also a beautiful place. In the far north, along the Baltic Sea, sandy coasts give way to ancient forests and rolling plains dotted with hundreds of lakes. Looming over nearly every landscape are the towers of medieval castles and the ruins of fortifications, some hundreds of years old and some barely more than fifty. Moving inland, the vast rolling plain is a patchwork of small farms, broken up by stretches of beautiful forests of oak and other deciduous trees, and cities and towns of every size and description.

Poland's diverse landscape includes everything from small farms, such as this one, to crowded cities and polluted industrial areas.

Toward Poland's southern border the elevation begins to rise as foothills give way to the northernmost peaks of the Carpathian Mountains, which stretch southeast of Poland almost to the Black Sea.

Poland is a land where the ancient and the modern rub shoulders. Many of its cities are built around charming historic centers, from which radiate outward the glass and steel skyscrapers of the business districts and, further beyond, miles of suburbs. Quaint villages dating from the first millennium are nestled within a stone's throw of communities that did not exist even a few decades ago. Farmers load

Old and new buildings stand side by side in Gdańsk. This peaceful coexistence of traditional and modern characterizes most aspects of Polish culture.

wheat and rye onto horse-drawn wagons, while smoke from nearby industrial plants wafts upward against the horizon to blend into the ever-present cloud of smog.

It is a land where the past is never far away, and human lives, with all their weaknesses and strengths, fragility and stubbornness, are played out against the backdrop of a seemingly eternal landscape. Over the great and ancient plains of Poland rolled the armies of the murderous dictators Hitler and Stalin, ushering in a bloody era from which the country has not yet fully recovered. In the filtered light of ancient oak trees, Polish resisters were shot, their bones later discovered in mass graves. Across the gray skies drifted ash from the Nazi concentration camps at Auschwitz, Majdanek, and Treblinka. Where spires of churches once reached from the plains toward the sky, only piles of rubble remained. Poland lay in ruins. But once again, the Poland of the mind remained alive.

REBUILDING AN INDEPENDENT NATION

In 1980, after forty years of repression, first under the Nazi army of Hitler's Germany, and then under the Communists, the independent and strong Poland which had endured as a dream in the minds of Poles once more began to emerge when workers at the Lenin shipyard in Gdańsk began a series of strikes against the communist-run government; they formed the first legally recognized union in Poland—Solidarność, or Solidarity. Over the next decade, the overwhelming will of the Polish people to determine their own destiny swept the Communists from power, and in 1990 an event occurred which was unthinkable even a decade before: Lech Walęsa, a former electrician and leader of Solidarity, became president of Poland.

It was an exciting time, and for a while anything seemed possible. But building a strong country from the ruins of communism has been more difficult than anyone could have imagined. In the 1980s and 1990s Poland's economy has remained very weak, its people unused to personal liberties such as free speech. Conflicting ideas about the future direction of Poland has led in recent years to divisiveness and political chaos. Transforming industries from state ownership under communism to private ownership in the new Poland has proven difficult when few Poles have money to invest in businesses. Turning inefficient, environmentally toxic mines and factories into clean and profitable ones has created mass unemployment and political unrest. On the positive side, Polish people's pride in their culture has resulted in a re-building program which has restored most historic areas leveled by Nazi bombs and artillery, and produced a vibrant arts scene equal to that anywhere in Europe.

CONTEMPLATING THE FUTURE

It has been a tumultuous and passionate decade, and Poland's course in the next few years is uncertain, except for the fact that it will be the Poles who determine it. Poland's current prime minister, Jerzy Buzek, is reported by the Associated Press as saying in a recent speech, "regardless of the effort and strain we wrestled with along the way, we can now say: It was worth it."[2]

His opinion is not shared by all. In fact, Buzek's popularity waned considerably in 1999, and he may not hold on to power long in the aftermath of his sweeping reforms of social security and health care, as well as his plans to sell off the railroads, the national airline, and utility companies to private investors. A growing number of Poles would like to see a return to communism at least in some aspects of their lives because they see no end to the chaos and decline in standard of living. Others are not so sure a return to communism is the solution, but are losing confidence that their leaders can find a way out of Poland's current problems.

However, Buzek's optimism seems to come from somewhere deep in the core of the Polish people. The struggle to create a new Poland is clearly "worth it" to its citizens. Despite its current problems, it is a nation whose true period of greatness may still lie ahead.

POLAND AND ITS NEIGHBORS

Poland lies in the middle of a huge expanse of low flatlands which stretch from Belgium through the Netherlands and northern Germany to the Polish border. There the elevation slowly begins to rise to form a rolling plain which stretches for thousands of miles north and east of Poland through the Baltic States and Belarus. This plain is characterized by open pasture lands, thick old forests and groves, and scattered lakes. In the south of Poland rise the Carpathian Mountains, including the High Tatras and other rugged ranges which form the border with the Czech Republic, Slovakia, and Ukraine.

Being in the middle of such a flat and thus easily traveled route between western Europe and central Asia, Poland has been visited over the centuries by many outsiders. Some of these outsiders wanted simply to establish trade routes or settle peaceably, but others have had different motives. With the rise of large and powerful nations around it, Poland became a stage on which the ambitions of other countries were played out. For centuries the borders of Poland shifted east and west, north and south, as empires such as Russia, Prussia (now Germany), Austria, and others maneuvered for control of Europe. For a while Poland was itself powerful enough to expand its territory far beyond its present borders, but for the most part it has had to fight, sometimes unsuccessfully, to avoid being swallowed up by other countries over the centuries.

Thus, though a visitor today might travel for miles over identical looking farmlands, and stop in village after village of blue-eyed, light-skinned people speaking Polish, the country has far more historical diversity than meets the eye. Likewise it has a great deal more geographical diversity than is evident on a map.

WIELKOPOLSKA

The region of Wielkopolska, meaning "Great Poland," is so named because it was where the country was born, and from which it expanded during the Piast dynasty at the end of the first millennium A.D. Located in central western Poland, this region ends at the Oder River, which forms the border with Germany.

Its most important city is Poznań, situated in the center of Wielkopolska. A major European industrial and trade center, Poznań annually hosts a famous international trade fair. In addition to a bustling present, Poznań also has a remarkable past. It dates from the ninth century when a fort on the Warta River grew into one of the largest castles in the region

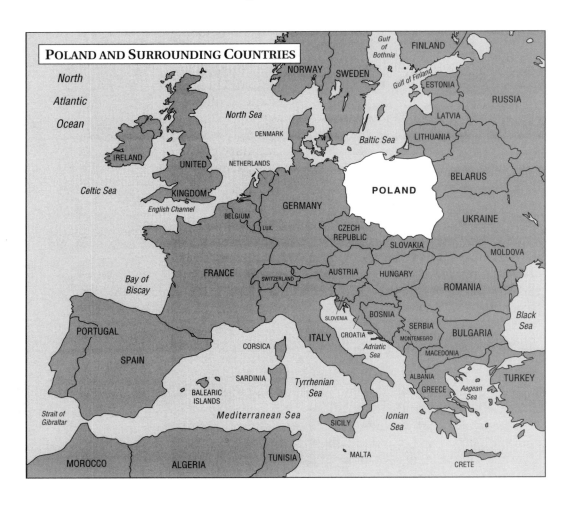

POLAND AND SURROUNDING COUNTRIES

and the surrounding town of Poznań became the capital of Wielkopolska. The town flourished culturally and economically because of its location: Here the east-west trade routes between Europe and Asia crossed the north-south routes linking Scandinavia with southern Europe.

The historical center of Poznań is Cathedral Island, named for the oldest church in Poland, built in A.D. 968. The cathedral contains the tombs of Mieszko I, the founder of Poland, and Boleslaw I, his son, its first crowned king. Another interesting historical site in Poznań is the Market Square, which contains many medieval style buildings and a beautiful urban park containing a large zoo and a lake famous for international canoeing and rowing regattas.

Poznań is situated in the middle of a deciduous forest typical of lowland Poland. Nearby Rogalin, a town by the Warta River, lies in a park on the edge of an oak forest which has more ancient oaks than any other forest in Europe, many of them over eight hundred years old. Three are named for the legendary founders of Poland, Bohemia, and Russia—Lech, Czech, and Rus, respectively.

Eastern Wielkopolska is an agricultural area, a flat plain with little woodland. Here many farmers still harvest their grain with pitchforks and horse-drawn wagons on hundreds of tiny farms. In this region is the town of Września, containing numerous memorials to Poles who gave their lives fighting against nineteenth-century efforts by Prussian occupiers to "Germanize" the population and eradicate Polish culture. One such historic site is a school where children went on strike in 1901 to demand that their religious education be in Polish rather than German.

Western Wielkopolska is renowned for its beautiful woods and lakes, formed by retreating glaciers during the Ice Age. Numerous castles, monasteries, and historic buildings from many different eras are scattered around this region, as well as an interesting maze of thirty miles of tunnels and above-ground fortifications used by the Germans against the Russians in World War II.

MALOPOLSKA

Southeast of Wielkopolska is the region of Malopolska, or "Little Poland." It has been called this since around A.D. 990

when it became an extension of Wielkopolska under Mieszko I. The name is not entirely accurate because Malopolska at one point was much larger than it is today, stretching beyond Lwów, now a city in Ukraine. Today Malopolska forms the Polish border with Ukraine to the east and Slovakia to the south.

Malopolska contains large tracts of ancient forest, now home to numerous national parks and reserves where wolves, bears, and bison still roam wild. Its southern region forms the northern end of the vast Carpathian Mountains which stretch southward beyond Poland into Romania, near the Black Sea. In Malopolska the Carpathians give way to foothills near the border with Slovakia, and then continue in a pattern of hills and valleys which characterize the rest of the region. The region is crisscrossed with rivers, the best known of which is the Vistula.

Malopolska has what most agree is one of the most beautiful and culturally rich cities in Europe: Kraków. In World War II the Poles surrendered it without a fight, in the hopes of preserving the city from German bombings. The strategy worked and Kraków was one of the few places in Poland to escape destruction. Kraków was important enough to have a cathedral by A.D. 1000. Twice in the thirteenth century it was invaded by the Tatars, fierce warriors whose mounted army was formed under the great Asian leader Genghis Khan. By 1384 the city had been rebuilt to include the first university in Poland, the Jagiellonian University, founded in 1364 and named after an early ruler of the combined kingdom of Poland and Lithuania. From 1038, when Wawel Castle was built, Kraków was the home of Polish kings and thus the national capital for almost six centuries. Its long history at the political center of Polish life, as well as its growth as a center for trade and a home for artisans from all over Europe, combine today to make a visit to Kraków a great cultural experience.

Kraków's Market Square is one of the largest medieval squares on the continent. At its center is the Cloth Hall, whose upper levels were

Kraków's stately Wawel Castle, built in 1038, was the home of Poland's monarchs for almost six hundred years.

REBUILDING HISTORIC POLAND

During World War II aerial bombardment and groundfire brought whole Polish cities toppling to the ground. With them fell a millennium of history. These bombings often served no specific military purpose such as destroying weapons or killing soldiers. Rather, historic districts all over Europe, usually in city centers, were deliberately targeted by both Nazis and Allied forces as a way of demoralizing nations and breaking their will to go on fighting.

Poland was one of the worst hit in this fashion. By the end of the war, in cities like Warsaw and Poznań hardly any buildings were left standing. After the war, a few Poles argued to build modern-looking cities over the rubble, but most people wanted to rebuild the historic districts of their cities exactly the way they had been. All over Poland, efforts were soon under way to research old photographs and historic records to determine the whole history of each building in the city center and reconstruct it from the same materials down to the last detail. In cities as old as those in Poland, many historic districts evolved over centuries and thus are a mix of architectural styles from different eras. A Renaissance-era upper floor, for example, was commonly built directly on top of a one-story medieval building, and thus the reconstructed buildings had to reflect multiple styles and use different building materials.

Fine examples of these reconstructed historic districts abound all over Poland in large cities like Warsaw and Poznań as well as smaller cities and towns. Thousand-year-old cathedrals, palaces, and market squares are actually, in one respect, as new as the skyscrapers that now overlook them. But no one would argue that these buildings are frauds simply because they are restored. They are the right buildings in the right places—Polish history reclaimed from the ashes.

actually built in the Renaissance, as were those of many other buildings in the square. Today the market origins of the square are still evident in the colorful stalls and arcade shops selling Polish handicrafts to tourists, amid the sounds of strolling musicians. Also on the square is the seven-hundred-year-old Church of St. Mary of the Assumption, from which a trumpeter sounds the hour without fail. From Market Square the Royal Way, lined with historic monuments and

THE TRUMPETER OF KRAKÓW

The market square in Kraków is dominated by the Mariacki, the Church of St. Mary of the Assumption, built in the fourteenth through sixteenth centuries. Every hour for the past seven hundred years a trumpeter has played the same tune from its towers. This practice commemorates a successful defense of Kraków against the Tatars. The watchman assigned to guard the town saw an approaching army of Tatars. When he began loudly playing the "Hejnal," a tune that served as a warning to the citizenry, he was killed by an arrow through the throat before he could finish. Today the trumpeter plays the same tune, stopping before the end of the tune with a broken-off high note, to signify the point at which the trumpeter was hit. This serves as a reminder of the historical bravery of the Poles, and for the same reason, the first few notes of the tune are played every morning on the radio stations of Poland to signal the beginning of the broadcast day.

The Mariacki Church in Kraków. A trumpeter plays from the tower of this church every hour, a tradition that has endured for centuries.

buildings, heads toward Wawel Hill and the royal palace, dating from the tenth century. The cathedral on Wawel Hill served as the coronation and burial site for most Polish rulers from the fourteenth century until the end of the monarchy around 1800.

Kazimierz, a section of Kraków, was for centuries an independent town governed by its Jewish residents. In 1941 all the Jews who lived elsewhere in Kraków and the surrounding area were forced to live in Kazimierz, which was the setting for the movie and book *Schindler's List*. The factory where the Jews who had been saved from the Nazis by Oskar Schindler worked still stands near the ghetto, although Plaszów, a labor camp outside town, has since been torn down.

Also in Malopolska are the towns of Sandomierz on the Vistula River and Jaroslaw on the San River. Considered to be among the most charming towns in Poland, they still retain a strong medieval aura. Sandomierz, like many other villages all over Poland was looted, bombed, and burned by the Nazis, then restored by local residents to look as it did before the war. However Sandomierz, like most other Polish villages, is not meant to be a tourist showcase but is a real working town. According to Polish travel writer Stanislaw Klos,

> [a]lthough much has been perfectly restored by skilled craftsmen, it is hard to conceal a certain urban shabbiness, but this is one of the things that makes many Polish towns so charming. Instead of sterile cleanliness, these old quarters successfully convey the impression of working communities where ordinary people still lead normal lives.[3]

The other side of the San River beyond Jaroslaw marks the point at which the Roman Catholic form of Christianity gives way to the Russian Orthodox. Churches in this area are topped with onion-domes and Ukrainian customs predominate. This area is also home to Zamość, whose Polish

The quaint town of Sandomierz, on the Vistula River in Malopolska, was destroyed during World War II and rebuilt by residents.

residents were expelled during World War II as part of Hitler's plan to establish model German communities on the Russian border. As a result, the old buildings were spared, but many of the inhabitants, particularly the Jews, were herded to the town square and shot, or sent to the nearby death camp at Belzec.

Besides Kraków, probably the best known city in Malopolska is Lublin, a cultural, trading, and educational center. It is home to the Katolicki Uniwersytet Ludowy (Catholic People's University or KUL), the only Catholic university in eastern Europe. The Nazis set up one of their largest extermination camps in Majdanek, just outside Lublin, where most of Lublin's forty thousand Jews were murdered.

KARPATY: THE HIGH TATRAS, BIESZCZADY, AND BESKIDY

The small Polish stretch of the Carpathian Mountains, the second largest mountain range in Europe after the Alps, is comprised of the High Tatras and two lower ranges, the Bieszczady and the Beskidy. The entire region was made into a national park earlier in this century, but many traditional villages remain. Among these villages is Zakopane, famous for tiny wooden houses elaborately carved in what is known as the Zakopane style. It is still home to the Górale, one of the many remaining small ethnic groups in Poland. This remote area became a center of intellectual life in the nineteenth century and continues to be an artists' colony today. It is also a winter sports center for skiers, and at one time hosted the winter Olympics.

SILESIA

Nestled in the southwest corner of Poland is the region of Upper and Lower Silesia. Beginning just west of Kraków, Upper Silesia is characterized by three sites that capture some of the best and the worst about Polish life in the twentieth century. The first is the area around the cities of Gliwice and Katowice, an area acknowledged to be one of the most polluted places in the world. The rivers and lakes are so damaged that the water cannot be used even in industry, and the landscape, seen through a thick haze of smog, is characterized by large heaps of refuse left from the mining of iron and coal.

The second site is Oświęcim, known to the world as Auschwitz, the death camp which is undoubtedly one of the

VESTIGES OF HORROR: THE DEATH CAMPS TODAY

The single most famous symbol of the Holocaust is the death camp of Auschwitz-Birkenau, but it was not by any means the only such camp in Poland. Hundreds of concentration camps existed across Europe, serving as places to round up prisoners while their fates were decided. From concentration camps, or directly from the ghettos, Jews and others were sent to death camps, which were little more than slaughterhouses.

A number of death camps are scattered across Poland. Most were built close to major cities so that when the ghettos were cleared, their residents would not have to be transported very far. Some of these camps are well known and others have faded into obscurity, at least for those whose loved ones did not suffer there. Camps other than Auschwitz-Birkenau are less visited and photographed not just because they are in more remote locations but also because some of them were nearly obliterated by the Nazis in an attempt to cover up their crimes when the war was ending.

One of these camps was Belzec, near the Ukrainian border. In 1943, the retreating Nazis bulldozed the site and planted trees over it. The estimated 600,000 people who died at Belzec are memorialized today at the site. Chelmno, near Lódź, has the dubious distinction of being the first death camp built in Poland. Approximately 340,000 people died there, but today only traces of the camp remain.

Sobibor and Treblinka are better known. Sobibor, near the Belarus border, was the site of an inmate revolt during which approximately 250 prisoners escaped. A quarter of a million people died at Sobibor, and a mound of ashes from their corpses is part of the memorial there. The Nazis bulldozed the site of Treblinka, roughly sixty miles north of Warsaw, and planted grass before Allied troops arrived, in an attempt to obliterate evidence of its existence. Treblinka today is the site of a Museum of Remembrance and a large memorial park. Small stones serve as markers for each of the 800,000 people who died there.

best-known symbols of Nazi atrocities. It is estimated that during World War II as many as 2 million people died in Auschwitz and the neighboring camp, Birkenau, of starvation, disease, and Zyklon B, the poison used in the gas chambers. The camps are now the Auschwitz-Birkenau museum and memorial. Visitors can view the ironic inscription "Arbeit Macht Frei" (Work Makes People Free) over one of the iron gates, stand where the trains deposited their loads of frightened Jews, and visit barracks where prisoners were housed. Some of the barracks now have exhibits designed to help visitors understand the enormity of the Holocaust. One room is entirely filled with hair shorn from prisoners' heads, and other rooms are filled with their clothing, shoes, eyeglasses, and other possessions.

The third site is Częstochowa, home of the Black Madonna, an icon which attracts thousands of visitors to the city, in the hope of cures from disease and relief from other problems. It serves as a symbol of the profound faith of Polish Catholics. Votive offerings from Pope John Paul II, himself a Pole, are displayed in the museum adjoining the church, which is full of cast-off crutches and other offerings to the Madonna.

THE BLACK MADONNA OF CZĘSTOCHOWA

Częstochowa, a small town in Upper Silesia, near Kraków, is an important place of pilgrimage for Polish Catholics. They come to see the Black Madonna, an icon housed in the Chapel of the Virgin Mary of Częstochowa. The picture of the mother of Jesus was originally created in Ukraine and brought to Silesia in 1382 by Prince Wladyslaw, although legends proclaim it was painted from life by Saint Luke on a wooden beam from Jesus' house in Nazareth. Chemical processes caused the white face of the Madonna to turn black, and because these processes were not understood, the change was seen as a divine sign. People began flocking to see the icon by the 1400s, and soon they were attributing miracles to it. These miracles include the legendary story of an attempted theft of the icon. As the thieves ran off with the icon, it became so heavy they could no longer carry it. Angry, they slashed the Virgin's face, which began to shed blood. Two scratches, said to represent the wounds, are visible today.

The Black Madonna has served as a symbol of the power of faith over the centuries. The church where it is housed is filled with cast-off crutches and offerings to the Madonna. Offerings from famous Poles, including early kings, Pope John Paul II, and Lech Wałęsa, the former president of Poland, are displayed in a nearby museum. The town is filled every day with pilgrims, many of whom are young. Mark Salter and Gordon McLachlan, in *Poland: The Rough Guide,* comment on "the number of excited teenagers in attendance, all treating the event with the expectation you'd find at an international rock concert."

Lower Silesia is west of Upper Silesia and borders Germany and the Czech Republic. Its major city is Wroclaw. Lower Silesia is typical of much of Poland in that the countryside is dotted with castles, monasteries, and old towns dating from the medieval, Gothic, and Renaissance eras. Unfortunately it is also typical of parts of Poland in other respects, in that heavy mining, primarily of copper, has blighted the landscape and fouled the air. Overall, Lower Silesia is a place of much charm, some of it destroyed by poor environmental practices during the communist era, which saw belching smokestacks as a sign of modernity and economic strength.

MAZOVIA

Mazovia stretches east from the area around Warsaw, Poland's capital, to the border with Belarus and Ukraine. Warsaw has a beautiful city center, with a medieval old town and many parks, as well as palaces, mansions, churches, and monuments. The beautiful Radziwill Palace, home of the Polish president since 1994, is a major Warsaw landmark. There the Warsaw Pact, a mutual cooperation and defense agreement between communist countries, similar to the North American Treaty Organization (NATO) between European countries and the United States, was signed in 1955. There also, talks between the communist government and the new union Solidarity took place in the 1980s. Nearby are tree-lined streets housing many of the foreign embassies and Warsaw University.

Warsaw's central district is the site of the Warsaw ghetto. During World War II, all 375,000 of the Jews of Warsaw, 30 percent of the city's overall population, were forced to live in a 1.5-square mile area, from which most were ultimately rounded up and sent to the death camp at Treblinka. In 1943 an uprising by the remaining Jews led to the ghetto's destruction by the Nazis in search of their hiding places. Today a memorial route commemorates the suffering and death in the ghetto, with a memorial at the site of the train platform where Jews and others were herded onto cattle cars, and a Monument to the Heroes of the Ghetto. In 1970 German chancellor Willy Brandt visited this memorial, kneeling at its base in recognition of the wrongs done to Poland by his country in World War II.

Visitors view the Warsaw Ghetto Monument, a tribute to the heroes of the ghetto.

In Poland, whether in city or countryside, one cannot go far without being reminded of recent history. Just outside Warsaw is Kampinoski Park, the largest national park in Poland. A beautiful preserve of rare birch trees, elks, and beavers, it was also where many Poles were secretly brought by the Nazis and shot. Nearby is the Modlin Fortress, built by the French emperor Napoléon when he invaded the region around 1800, and expanded by the Russians during their occupation of Poland at the end of World War II. With a perimeter of 8,650 feet, it is the longest building in Europe, and can house as many as twenty-six thousand soldiers at one time.

Surrounding Warsaw are many charming market towns, many of them bearing names of battles in the various wars for control of Poland through the centuries. The only other large city in Mazovia is Bialystok, origin of the bagel-like bialy. The architecture in this mostly rural area reflects Russian influence and traces of the many trading cultures which passed through the area. Along the Polish border is the Bialowieza National Park, a forest which was once the private domain of princes and kings, and which today is still off limits to visitors unless accompanied by a guide, to preserve the wild horses, bears, wolves, and other rare species that live there.

West of Warsaw is Lódź, the second largest city in Poland. It is an important center of textile manufacturing and chemical industries. It was a major center of Jewish population, housing the largest Jewish cemetery in Europe. As elsewhere in Poland, the Jewish population of this city was virtually eliminated by the Nazis, who sent them to their death at nearby Chelmno. Surrounding Lódź is a mixture of quaint old villages, beautiful moated castles, and unattractive industrial towns.

NORTHERN POLAND

Northern Poland stretches along the Baltic Coast between Germany and a small patch of Russian Federation land around the city of Kaliningrad. It consists of West and East Pomerania, and a cluster of small regions called Warmia, Mazury, and Suwalszczyzna. Pomerania has changed hands even more often than other parts of Poland in the last eight hundred years, and West Pomerania was only restored to Poland recently when the reunification of East and West Germany shifted Poland's border westward.

One of the major landmarks in northern Poland is the city of Gdańsk, known formerly under its German name, Danzig.

Gdańsk was nicknamed the "Pearl of the Baltic" because its port was so important over the centuries. Gdańsk is best known today as the place where the political movement Solidarity was born. Gdańsk is situated on the Bay of Gdańsk, which is formed by a spit of land known as the Hel Peninsula, home to many small fishing villages. The border with the Russian Federation lies along the eastern stretch of the Bay of Gdańsk.

WOLF'S LAIR

The small town of Gierloz in the Mazurian Lakes region of northern Poland is the site of a huge secret headquarters, called Wilczy Szaniec, or Wolf's Lair, from which Hitler conducted the Nazi war effort for three years. Between 1940 and 1942 eighty buildings were erected, including seven huge bunkers whose twenty-five-foot thick concrete walls were designed to protect the lives of Hitler and his staff in the event of direct hits by bombs or heavy artillery. To keep the site from being visible from the air it was covered by a camouflage screen made of vegetation matching the current season.

Hitler actually lived at Wolf's Lair for three years, leaving only briefly to make public appearances. However, despite such efforts to protect him, it was at Wolf's Lair that his life was almost ended in an assassination attempt. Near the end of the war, a concerned member of Germany's nobility, Claus Schenk von Stauffenberg, masterminded a conspiracy to kill Hitler, seize control of the army, and surrender so that no more lives would be lost. He used his security clearance to smuggle a bomb in his briefcase into Wolf's Lair and leave it under a conference table next to Hitler. The bomb went off after Stauffenberg left, but someone had thought the briefcase was in the way and moved it behind a pillar. Hitler suffered only a torn eardrum, but four people were killed in the massive explosion. Stauffenberg and the other conspirators were executed, and using the assassination attempt as a pretext, Hitler had five thousand people he considered enemies killed as co-conspirators.

Today, visitors can peer into the bunkers and see the staff living quarters and the operations room where Stauffenberg's assassination attempt on Hitler was made.

Inland from the bay is a huge fortification, Malbork Palace, a reminder of the power of the Teutonic Knights, a group of independent warriors who set up their own country in Pomerania in the 1300s. Still further inland is the university city of Toruń, home to Nicolaus Copernicus University, named after the sixteenth-century Polish astronomer. It was in the East Pomeranian town of Frombork, near the Russian border, that he wrote his treatise showing that the earth and the planets revolved around the sun.

Like Pomerania, the regions of Mazury, Warmia, and Suwalszczyzna have been swapped between Poland and other powers many times over the centuries, beginning with the Teutonic Knights in the fourteenth century. Portions of the region only became part of Poland again after World War II. The geographical feature of greatest note is the Mazurian Lake district, dotted with close to one thousand small lakes, many connected by canals popular with canoers and motorboaters. The region is so inaccessible that Adolf Hitler chose it as the location of his huge secret military complex, Wolf's Lair.

Thus it is clear that in Poland, history and geography are tightly linked. Characteristics of the land have played a role in human events, and these events have often in turn left their marks on the land. Wherever one goes in this country at the heart, and some say the soul, of Europe, the whole history of its people seems to be continually retold.

2

A Nation Rises and Vanishes

From the Stone Age until the present time, Poland has been home to various groups of people. Archaeological and other evidence reveals that the great plain between the Baltic Sea and the Carpathian Mountains began to be populated by the ancestors of modern Poles, the Slavs, around A.D. 375. The Slavs had not come by choice but had been pushed north and west from their original homes by more aggressive tribes. Thus, from the very beginning the history of Poland has been shaped by pressures from the outside. Over the centuries many other countries have kept their eye on Poland, waiting for the right moment to claim it for themselves. In recent centuries they have, for the most part, succeeded.

The early Slavs gradually spread out in small communities over the plains and southern mountains of today's Poland. Because they had no central ruler or main city, these regions often became known by the name of the group who settled there such as the Ślęzanie and the Mazowianie, who gave their names to the regions of Silesia and Mazovia. These regional Slavic cultures had enough in common, however, to make alliances easy to achieve, and evidence suggests that the early history of Poland was relatively free of conflict among the Slavs. Later conflicts were almost always with outside powers seeking to suppress or destroy Polish culture and take over the land.

The Piast Dynasty

By 900, the various Slavic groups were organized into protective alliances and had built small, fortified towns which served as centers of trade. Life in Poland was fairly typical of Europe in this era. Most people did not identify with any entity larger than their village. Kingdoms usually evolved as a result of a strong personality able to pull distant people together either by force or by persuasion. This happened in the late tenth century in Poland with Mieszko, the leader of the Polanie people and the legendary founder of the Piast dynasty. Soon most of the southern Slavic groups, which Mieszko had persuaded to form a confederation for protection against non-Slavs, were calling themselves Polanie, or Poles, and referring to their land as Wielkopolska, or Great Poland.

Mieszko soon realized that his loose conglomeration of Slavic groups would be no match for the powerful Holy Roman Empire, which was centered south of Poland in Austria, and had a history of invading countries on the pretext of spreading Christianity. He thus decided that the best thing to do was to join the enemy rather than fight it. Mieszko converted to Christianity in 966 and had all of his subjects baptized. He then married the sister of the neighboring duke of Bohemia, creating a friendly alliance along his southern border. Presumably these acts were not done from any deep religious convictions or love but rather to achieve his overall goal of creating a stronger Slavic empire. In the next few years Mieszko was able to expand his reach, pulling the neighboring region around the Vistula River into his empire as the region of Malopolska, or Little Poland. He also brought Silesia, home to yet another Slavic group, under his control.

Although Mieszko had managed to keep vast stretches of Slav-inhabited land out of the hands of more aggressive rulers, this collection of territories was still not recognized as an independent country. Though subsequently he became known as Mieszko I, implying that he was the first of several kings named Mieszko, in fact he remained nothing more than a powerful noble at the time of his death. His son, Boleslaw I, was able to finish the process of creating the nation of Poland. On a visit to Boleslaw in 1000, Otto III, the Holy Roman Emperor, crowned Boleslaw as king of a sovereign nation, thus announcing that he would not attempt to take his land. Boleslaw arranged for a

Mieszko I, founder of the Piast dynasty.

THE MEDIEVAL CATHOLIC CHURCH

"Mieszko's baptism in A.D. 965 was the first step in the formation of the single most important element in modern Polish culture," according to Norman Davies in *Heart of Europe: A Short History of Poland.* The church, Davies points out, "provided a stronger bond of continuity in the life of the nation than the fluctuating rule of the Piast princes, or the fragmented history of the Piast state." Davies explains the important role of the church in its early days:

> [T]he Church stood at the centre, not just of politics, but of medieval consciousness. It . . . explained the links not only of the King to his Crown, but also of every man and woman to their ruler and to the universe. It was the fount of all knowledge. It provided the literate clerks who ran the [government offices], and the Latin language with which all educated men worked. It enjoyed a monopoly in formal education. Its monasteries were the research laboratories of the day. Its prelates combined the powers of barons, ministers, and diplomats. Its friars and nuns were the teachers and social workers. Its faithful, who accepted the Faith with a finality inconceivable in the present age, comprised the overwhelming mass of Poland's population. It is usually said that Piast Poland adopted Christianity. It may be more accurate to say that the Catholic Church adopted Poland.

second coronation by the pope himself in 1025, after which there was no doubt that Poland was an independent nation and Boleslaw was its king.

In the years between the two coronations, Boleslaw had been busy expanding Poland's territory. He established control farther north in Mazovia and Pomerania, began pushing west into Bohemia (now in the Czech Republic), and east into Ukraine. Where only one generation before there had been no more than a scattering of small, independent Slavic communities, by the time of Boleslaw's second coronation, Poland had become a large country dominating central Europe.

Mieszko and Boleslaw I were the first leaders in the Piast dynasty, but over the course of the next two centuries, Poland, like most of Europe in the Middle Ages, dissolved back into small territories ruled by powerful dukes, many related to the Piasts by blood or marriage. Life in rural communities continued much as it always had, revolving around seasonal crops and the Catholic Church, to which the Poles had become sincerely devoted in the years since Mieszko. But during the twelfth and thirteenth centuries several developments at opposite ends of Poland would have profound effects on the future of the country.

Immigration and the Rise of the Cities

The region of Malopolska, with its main city, Kraków, became the political and cultural center of Poland in the Middle Ages. Situated along the main trade route between Vienna and the eastern cities of Kiev and Byzantium (now Istanbul), because of overpopulation and other problems elsewhere in Europe,

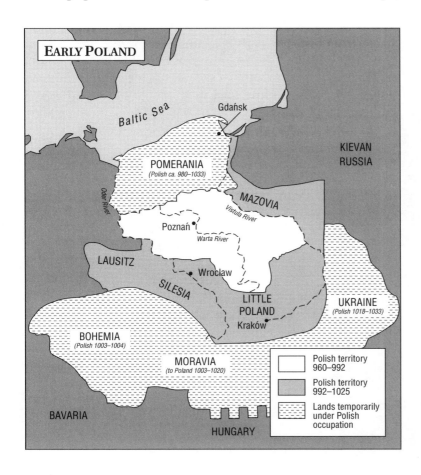

Malopolska became a magnet for immigrants. Among these immigrants were thousands of Jews who found the Slavs far more tolerant than people elsewhere. Kraków thus became one of the centers of Jewish civilization in Europe, and remained so until World War II.

From the beginning, Jews occupied an unusual position in Poland. They coexisted with Christians with few of the flare-ups of anti-Semitism, hatred toward Jews, that characterized the rest of Europe. Still, Christian and Jewish communities remained distinct and separate. As a result it was never clear whether Jews were Poles, or whether they constituted a permanent but still foreign group in Poland. This lack of clarity about the nationality of Jews and later about other non-ethnic Poles would have important consequences in the centuries to come.

The interior of a fifteenth-century synagogue in Kraków. Since the Middle Ages, Kraków was a haven for Jews, who found a relatively peaceful niche in Polish society.

Jews and other immigrants came to Kraków skilled in crafts and in running businesses. Soon this part of Poland became commercially prosperous and more advanced culturally than any of the surrounding areas. Other cities such as Wroclaw and Poznań, in the western regions closest to Germany, followed Kraków's example and also prospered.

During this era, the overall population patterns of today's Poland began to take shape.

THE TEUTONIC ORDER OF KNIGHTS

While modern cities were emerging in southern Poland, in northern Poland modernization was still far off. The medieval system in which warrior knights pledged service to a powerful ruler was enjoying a resurgence through the Teutonic Knights, an army of Germans founded in 1198 which fought in the Crusades to retake the Holy Land from the Muslims. A few years later, at the end of the Crusades, the knights became mercenaries, an army for hire, who used their heroic reputation to put an air of religious respectability into whatever quarrels they were hired to help settle.

In 1226, Duke Conrad of Mazovia became their employer. Mazovia had been under attack by the Prussians and Lithuanians, and Conrad wanted the Teutonic Knights to help defend the

THE TEUTONIC KNIGHTS

The Order of St. Mary of the Germans in Jerusalem, better known as the Teutonic Knights, was founded in 1198 by the Hohenstaufen emperors of medieval Germany. It served as one of the battle units sent to the Holy Land to try to get Jerusalem back from the Muslims. After the Crusades, the Teutonic Knights were not disbanded; instead they were permitted by the Catholic Church to hire themselves out to certain favored feudal lords who needed additional trained soldiers. Sometimes they were paid money, but in the case of Duke Conrad of Mazovia, the payment was a patch of land in northern Poland near Toruń. Conrad thought that the knights would remain loyal to him as sovereign of the entire region in which their land was situated, but they did not, and instead used the land as a base to expand their holdings.

The Teutonic Knights, immediately recognizable by their white cloak emblazoned with a black cross, were very well organized. They were headed by an elected Grand Master who served for life. There were commanders-in-chief for each region as well as castle commanders and knight-priests, responsible for the churches.

Once the knights abandoned their life as a roaming army and settled in to be landowners, they fared remarkably well. They cultivated farmlands and developed aggressive trade strategies with other port cities in the Hanseatic League, an international trading alliance. Their efforts made them rich; they used their wealth to support the arts and literature and to build magnificent castles such as the one at Malbork near the Baltic coast. The power of the knights was not broken until the Napoleonic wars, but even today the order survives, with headquarters in Vienna.

more remote regions of his territory. Their payment was a portion of the land they had defended. Dissatisfied with that, they moved north and established themselves as the rulers in the region along the Baltic Sea, including Gdańsk, which they renamed Danzig. The Teutonic Knights had thus succeeded in establishing a German presence the full length of the Polish coast. This was to be the beginning of centuries of mutual dislike between the Poles and the Germans, the Poles viewing the Germans as aggressive and self-impressed, and the Germans seeing the Poles as culturally inferior and weak.

The shift in roles of the Teutonic Knights from roving military to rulers of an independent state along the Baltic was disastrous to the Poles. The Poles had lost their access to the coast and thus could not develop ports during the time when international sea trade was beginning to transform Europe. The city of Danzig became one of the most important Baltic ports and it remained in the hands of Germans for hundreds of years. Furthermore, the Teutonic Knights began invading the lands they had once been hired to defend, and by the mid-1300s they controlled large sections of Wielkopolska. Poland, which up to then had viewed itself as a growing power, saw its borders shrink and suffered the first of many losses it would endure over the next few centuries.

Marienburg Castle in Malbork was the headquarters of the Teutonic Knights from 1309 to 1457.

THE REVIVALS OF THE PIASTS

The loss of the Baltic coast to the Teutonic Knights was the unforeseen consequence of a decision made two centuries

before. In 1138, when Piast ruler Boleslaw III died, his will dissolved the nation into four dukedoms, one for each of his sons. This decision weakened Poland, but by the thirteenth century, as the Teutonic Knights gobbled up more and more land, support for a reunified Poland grew. In 1320 a smaller Kingdom of Poland was reestablished under Wladyslaw I. Wladyslaw I was a man with no particular leadership skills. As a ruler he was unmemorable, but his son, Kazimierz III, the last of the Piast kings, is one of the reasons the Piast name still is remembered with pride in Poland. According to historians Waldemar Paclawski and Alfred Horn, "It was said of this king that he found a Poland built of wood, and left it built of stone."[4]

Kazimierz III, known as Kazimierz the Great, might today be called a master of public relations and marketing. He set out to turn Kraków into a grand city, complete with a university and impressive buildings, to send the message to western Europe that Poland was their cultural and commercial equal. He encouraged migration, particularly of skilled Jews, and passed a law in 1346 specifically outlawing discrimination against them. This contrasted markedly with the rest of Europe, where the Jews were often blamed for social problems and even natural disasters such as the bubonic plague that ravaged Europe at the time. Kazimierz also demonstrated Poland's modernity by introducing a stable national currency, establishing a constitution, writing down Poland's laws, and creating an administrative structure by which the nation's provinces could be centrally governed. Under Kazimierz, Poland once again gained the respect of other nations as well as the Catholic Church, which for the first time allowed Poland to appoint its own bishops rather than sending bishops from elsewhere.

Kazimierz wanted to strengthen the borders of Poland, and he did this in two ways. First, he built a number of impressive, fortified castles in the border regions of the country. Second, he bowed to several neighboring powers in a farsighted move to avoid future conflict. He surrendered Silesia to the king of Bohemia in exchange for that king's giving up his long-standing claim to be the true and lawful ruler of Poland, thus avoiding war on the southern border. In the north, Kazimierz acknowledged the Teutonic State, and thus removed any excuse the Teutonic Knights might give for invading northern Poland. This left Kazimierz free to invade the east, into parts of Ruthenia, a region along Poland's eastern border. Thus, when Kazimierz died in 1370, the boundaries of Poland had shifted once again to the east, but the country was on solid footing in the international community as a strong, independent nation.

THE JAGIELLONIANS

Kazimierz died childless, and in the years that followed, fights over the crown of Poland were to have far-reaching effects on eastern Europe. The closest relative to Kazimierz was his nephew, Louis of Anjou, the king of Hungary, and thus the crowns of the two countries were briefly united. However, upon the death of Louis, the nobles of Poland decided they preferred to have one of his younger children, Jadwiga, as their queen, rather than the heir-apparent, another of his daughters. Thus, the other daughter became queen of Hungary and Jadwiga became queen of Poland in 1384. It is unusual that nobles could successfully choose a ruler, and the coronation of Jadwiga shows the growth in power of the Polish nobility, a development that would ultimately have disastrous consequences.

The nobles' choice of Jadwiga also had a short-range positive effect. When Jadwiga married Wladyslaw Jagiello, grand duke of Lithuania, the joint kingdom of Poland and Lithuania—known as the "Two Kingdoms"—became one of the most powerful alliances in Polish history, giving Poland access to the Baltic Sea once again. Their combined strength was enough to risk war against the Teutonic State, and the joint kingdom crushed the order of Teutonic Knights altogether in 1466. During the two hundred years of the Two Kingdoms, in many respects Lithuania and Poland came to see themselves as one nation and one people.

THE REPUBLIC OF NOBLES

During the same two hundred years, the nobility, which had flexed its muscles by elevating Jadwiga to the throne, increased its power. When the last Jagiellonian ruler, Zygmunt August, died childless in 1572, the nobility announced the establishment of the Republic of Nobles. It would have as its ruler someone elected by them, who, according to writers Mark Salter and Gordon McLachlan, would be "forced to sign a document which reduced him to a managerial servant of the nobility."[5]

Although electing a leader and having the power to remove an unsatisfactory one might sound quite ahead of its time, the nobles' motives were not farsighted at all. In fact, historians have noted that despite the fact that almost 10 percent of Poles (the very large noble class) could actually vote—an astonishingly high percentage for the times—the net result was a society that was more old-fashioned than any other in Europe. The landed nobles, especially the ones in the far-flung regions of Ruthenia and Lithuania, wanted to live luxurious lives without any constraints; the penniless ones who had been awarded hastily created noble titles as a reward for war service wanted a chance to turn their title into land and fortune. Both saw their chances of staying ahead lying in a system which enabled them to make all the decisions.

REPUBLIC OF TWO NATIONS IN 1550

Adding to their powers were the Right of Resistance, which enabled the nobles to fire a king they did not like, and the liberum veto, which enabled even one "no" vote to defeat any proposal. In some sessions the Sejm, or Polish parliament, was unable to pass even a single law. According to historian Norman Davies, during the thirty year reign of one king, August III, "only one session of the [Sejm] succeeded in passing any legislation at all."[6]

On the nobles' lands, however, farmers were living lives of desperate poverty, and towns were going bankrupt when people stopped having goods to buy and sell. According to Paclawski and Horn, "The aristocratic families . . . ruled like little kings in their provinces and hardly wasted a second's thought on the well-being of the state."[7] Rather than building a strong nation, the nobles were destroying it by their own selfishness.

This hidden decay was noticed by the growing powers all around them: Russia to the east, Turkey to the south, Ger-

Polish nobles in 1600 gather in Wola, a small village near Warsaw, to elect a king. The Republic of Nobles, established in 1572, had the power to both elect and remove leaders.

many to the west, and Sweden to the north. Although some of the elected kings, such as Stefan Báthory (1576–1586) were actually good choices, their hands were tied by the nobility's unwillingness to tax itself even to protect the country from invasion. In the sixteenth and seventeenth centuries, Poland was engaged in near constant wars, winning a few battles but gradually losing ground. The Republic of Two Nations, as the kingdom of Poland and Lithuania came to call itself, had its last military victory over the Turks in the Battle of Vienna in 1683. After this point, the Polish nobility saw the inevitable collapse of their "republic," and began to align themselves with the foreign powers that were waiting for a chance to take over Poland.

THE SILENCE OF THE NOBLES

By 1700 the elections of Polish rulers were orchestrated largely by foreigners. Russia conspired to elect Augustus Wettin, who was deposed in 1704 in favor of a candidate backed by the Swedes. Augustus was reinstated in 1710, and the Russian influence grew. In 1717, known as the year of the Silent Sejm, the nobles kept quiet while Russian-backed proposals took away any chance of changing the constitution to shift power away from the nobles, who were by now completely under Russian control. According to noted historian Norman Davies, the Silent Sejm "imposed a protectorate over Polish life which could effectively obstruct all movement toward [r]eform and independence."[8]

In 1763, the Russians ensured the election of Stanislaw-August Poniatowski. Poniatowski was a former lover of the Russian empress or czarina Catherine the Great, and the Russians assumed he would be as willing a puppet as Wettin had been. But Poniatowski had a mind of his own and he did everything he could to bring Poland back to life as an independent country. He aroused in the Poles a sense of nationalism and encouraged the development of grassroots movements to keep Poland free. He forced the Sejm to act with at least some independence from Russia and tried to reform the tax system to create a war fund in the event of a Russian invasion.

Poniatowski's fears were realized when the Russian army invaded Poland to put down rebellions against its influence. But Russia was facing potentially bigger problems by the mid-1700s than a few stubborn Polish nationalists. Both Prussia (today's Germany) and Austria had strong rulers with large armies, and the only buffer between the three countries was Poland. A continued Russian policy of putting down rebellions in Poland might antagonize the Poles enough to enter an alliance with either Austria or Prussia. Czarina Catherine the Great was finally persuaded that the only way to ensure Russia's continued control over at least some of Poland, and thus to maintain the balance of power between the three countries, was to agree to Prussia's proposal to divide large sections of Poland between the three powers.

THE PARTITIONS OF POLAND

In 1772 the first partition of Poland was achieved. Austria, Prussia, and Russia simply announced that territory along their borders with Poland, 30 percent of Poland's land, was now theirs. Centuries of rule by self-serving nobles had left Poland bankrupt and unable to govern itself or tax itself for an army, so there was nothing it could do to stop the surrounding powers from taking what they wanted. Stung by this free fall in its national fortune, Poland acted quickly to reform itself, hoping thus to retain its identity and perhaps its very existence. According to Paclawski and Horn,

> In the legislative period of the Sejm, from 1788 to 1792, the whole political system was restructured and an army of 100,000 soldiers was recruited. Citizens were granted full civic rights and on 3 May 1791 the first modern constitution in all Europe was proclaimed. This new constitution granted political power to the citizens, allowed the cities self-determination and afforded legal protection to the peasants.[9]

Poland was the first modern democracy, but this was to prove only a brief interlude.

Catherine the Great was truly alarmed as the impotent country next door had turned seemingly overnight into a democracy. All over Europe monarchies were falling or threatened by revolutions, and Catherine must have won-

A British cartoon from 1774 satirizes the first partition of Poland. Seated from left to right, ready to carve up the Polish "cake," are Louis XV of France, Catherine II of Russia, Holy Roman Emperor Leopold II, and Frederick William II of Prussia.

TADEUSZ KOŚCIUSZKO

Tadeusz Kościuszko, famous as a general in both the American and Polish armies, began his career by studying military engineering and fortifications at the Warsaw Royal Military College. His training was cut short when he had to flee to Paris after trying to elope with a general's daughter. He continued on from Paris to America to fight in the Revolutionary War on the side of the colonists. He used his training to plan the strategy in the victorious defense of Saratoga, after which he was asked to design and supervise the building of the fortifications at West Point, and to assist in the blockade of Charleston. When the war was over, Kościuszko was made an honorary American citizen and a brigadier general in the U.S. Army.

He returned to Poland where he had trouble getting a military appointment because of a scandal involving yet another general's daughter. Eventually, before the last partition of Poland, he was given a chance to command and became famous as the leader of Kościuszko's Uprising in 1794, winning a victory against Russia at Raclawice with an army of peasants carrying only their scythes.

In 1796 he traveled again to the United States, where he was welcomed as a hero, and struck up a friendship with Thomas Jefferson. He also bought some land to farm, but soon returned to France in the hopes that he could persuade Napoléon to assist in the liberation of Poland. When Napoléon was vague about his commitment to help, Kościuszko sat out the Napoleonic wars, and later when he was approached by the Russian czar to help in the running of the Congress Kingdom, he again refused when his conditions to ensure the people's freedom were not accepted. Kościuszko died in Switzerland in 1817. True to his principles to the last, his will dictated that the proceeds from the sale of his American land be used to buy the freedom of slaves, including some of Jefferson's.

Tadeusz Kościuszko

dered whether her own throne might not be next. Catherine was able to apply her muscle to the Polish nobles still obliged to Russia, and after a few months of resistance, the Sejm annulled the new constitution and agreed to a second partition of Poland. This time the Austrians got nothing

PARTITIONS OF POLAND

LIVONIA

COURLAND

Baltic Sea

SAMOGITIA

TO RUSSIA

RUSSIAN

ERMLAND

Gdańsk (1793)

EAST PRUSSIA

LITHUANIA

WHITE RUSSIA

EMPIRE

POMERANIA

WEST PRUSSIA

TO PRUSSIA

NEW EAST PRUSSIA

SOUTH PRUSSIA

SILESIA

WESTERN GALICIA

POLESIE

VOLHYNIA

UKRAINE

TO AUSTRIA

NEW SILESIA

GALICIA AND LODOMERIA

PODOLIA

First Partition (1772)
Second Partition (1793)
Third Partition (1795)

HUNGARY

TURKISH EMPIRE

more, the Russians annexed the rest of Ruthenia in today's Ukraine, and the Prussians took Wielkopolska, sections of Mazuria in the north, and the port of Danzig (Gdańsk).

Poland was dismembered, but not yet entirely defeated. In 1794 a former American Revolutionary War hero, General Tadeusz Kościuszko, started an uprising in Kraków which quickly spread across the nation. A Polish peasant force armed only with scythes routed the Russian army at Raclawice, and this victory fanned further uprisings. But these efforts, however heroic, must have seemed a bit like flies bothering a lion. The superpowers had soon had enough of Poland. In 1795, they agreed among themselves to a third and final partition of Poland which divided all the remaining territory in Poland among the three powers. In 1798 the three powers signed a side treaty that removed even the name of Poland from any maps. The nation of Poland had simply ceased to exist.

THE STRUGGLE FOR SOVEREIGNTY: 1800–1918

As the nineteenth century began, Poles no longer lived in Poland although they had not gone anywhere. Poland had not been invaded by an army, the Poles had not lost a war, joined a federation, or agreed to be annexed for protection, but they still had lost their country. On the surface things looked the same—the sun rose and set every day over the same farms, churches, houses, fields, cities, and roads that had always been there. However, the partitions meant that people who formerly lived in Poland now lived in either Austria, Prussia, or Russia. The word *Poland* was not even to be spoken. Names of cities were changed to reflect the new language that would be spoken there—Poznań became Posen, Warszawa became Warsaw. School instruction was to be in the new "native" language, and the focus was to be on the history and culture of the Poles' new country. Particularly in the Russian and Prussian partitions, the goal was to do away with Polish language, culture, and pride as quickly as possible.

The fact that there is a Poland today is testament to the failure of the partitioners to achieve that goal. According to historian Norman Davies, "For most of the period, 'Poland' was just an idea—a memory from the past, or a hope for the future."[10] Every Pole—whether he or she stayed at home, joined a foreign army, or immigrated to the United States, France, or elsewhere—lived in a foreign country. But during the nineteenth century, Poles came to realize that where they lived physically was not as important as where they lived mentally. In that respect, they all still lived in Poland.

LIFE IN THE THREE PARTITIONS

Life in each of the three partitions was different. The attitude of the partitioning powers toward the Poles varied, as did styles of government and leadership. Russia, for example, saw the Poles as part of the same ethnic group as themselves, all fellow Slavs, and saw itself as the great leader and protector of the Slavic people against threats from western Europe. Poles living in the Russian partition found it advantageous, at least at the beginning, to be part of a more advanced industrial society than their own. Huge new markets opened up for Polish products and they gained access to a welcome network of railroads and factories. Many Poles embraced the changes, sniffing at how backward they had been before the partitions. A new kind of Polish aristocracy emerged among those non-nobles who became rich through success in business. But still, according to Norman Davies, "the modest rise of prosperity could not indefinitely compensate for resentments caused by the presence of a colossal garrison [of military troops], the despotism of petty officials, and the irrational hostility to all things Polish."[11] In other words, the humiliation of being treated like second-class citizens in their own country made even the improvements in their lives a bitter pill to swallow.

In western Poland, now officially part of Prussia, the situation was quite different. No common culture could be claimed, and the Germans felt themselves superior in every way to the Poles. They tried to force German culture on the Poles rather than allow them to adapt to it, but they soon found that, according to Davies, "the sturdy Polish peasantry of Prussia, mobilized by a militant Catholic clergy, was thoroughly disaffected, and . . . determined to defend its Polishness with a will."[12] Hostility between Poles and Germans grew steadily throughout the nineteenth century.

In Austrian Poland, called Galicia, the Poles' situation was a little better. The rulers of what was then Austria-Hungary were having difficulty holding their empire together, and they simply demanded loyalty from the Poles in exchange for a substantial amount of independence. Thus, in the southern regions of the former Poland, life remained in many respects much the same as it had been before the partitions. According to Davies,

SCHOOLING IN PARTITIONED POLAND

In the Prussian and Russian parts of Poland, the officials charged with overseeing the education of Polish youth went to extremes to destroy any sense of Polish identity and pride. Anyone who spoke Polish in school was subject to expulsion. Books in Polish were banned. Polish teachers had to speak only Russian or German to the children, and were dismissed if caught speaking Polish. In Warsaw in the 1880s a decision was reached to permit the study of certain approved literary works by Poles, but these were presented as foreign literature, and they were taught only in Russian translation. This would be the equivalent of having American students read Spanish translations of Mark Twain or Maya Angelou, to create the impression that they were Spanish authors.

Despite the serious consequences of defiance, Poles found many ways to educate themselves about Polish culture. For example, groups calling themselves welfare societies circulated books secretly; and an underground university called the Flying University, founded by a woman, Jadwiga Szczawińska, held classes in secret and constantly changing classrooms on subjects relating to Polish culture and history. By the time the partitions ended no one was alive who had ever lived in a country named Poland, but as a result of the efforts of the secret groupsJJ, Polish identity was still strong.

Galicia was far and away the poorest of the three partitions, with little industry and acute overpopulation in the countryside. It was controlled for the most part by conservative Polish landowners whose manipulations of the [government] were a standing joke. But a relaxed and nonchalant atmosphere gave scope for cultural enterprise.[13]

In Galicia, universities such as the Jagiellonian University in Kraków, the oldest in Poland, continued to promote Polish culture, and theaters and publishing houses were only mildly censored. Schools continued to promote a Polish identity among new generations of children. Thus, at least in one region, some sense of the existence of Poland on Polish soil was maintained.

DECADES OF DISAPPOINTMENTS

For most Poles, however, the nineteenth century was a brutal and disappointing time. Other countries such as France and the United States had thrown off monarchies in favor of rule by the citizens. Commoners such as Napoléon had risen to power in place of kings. Noble birth no longer was the only means to have wealth and status in society. Individuals could at least in theory create the kind of lives they wanted. All of this could not happen for the Poles, who were still controlled by powerful monarchs, and thus seemed stuck in a bygone era.

During the nineteenth century Poles participated in the major events happening in Europe, but they did so as foreigners. According to Davies, "there were Poles on every barricade in Europe, from Munich to Transylvania, from the Roman Republic to the Paris Commune. But the tangi-

A view of Warsaw in 1779, when the city was still part of Poland. The partitions would swallow all of Poland by 1795.

ble benefits for Poland were meagre."[14] For example, many Poles joined Napoléon's army, hoping that if they helped Napoléon defeat Prussia and Russia he would return Poland to them as a reward. The Polish Legions, formed in Italy under General Jan Henryk Dąbrowski from Polish deserters from other armies, sang a battle song showing this hope, a song which in 1926 became the Polish national anthem:

> Poland has not perished yet
> So long as we shall live.
> That which foreign force has seized
> We at swordpoint shall retrieve.
> March, march, Dąbrowski!
> From Italy to our Polish land.
> Let us now unite the nation
> Under thy command.[15]

Napoléon did reward the Poles after he defeated Prussia by returning some Polish territory around Warsaw and renaming it the Duchy of Warsaw. Although it had a Polish administration and its own army and constitution, Napoléon kept the duchy under his tight control and during its brief life it never constituted a revived Poland. After Napoléon was defeated, all three partitioning powers attended the Congress of Vienna (1814–1815). There they bowed to the disapproval of countries such as Great Britain and France about the partitions. The Congress of Vienna did not undo the partitions, but it determined that a separate Polish kingdom, called the Congress Kingdom, would be established in central Poland, to be controlled by the Russian czar. Kraków was also made a small independent republic, simply because the partitioners could not agree who should get it.

The Congress Kingdom was a sham from the start. Polish rights under the kingdom's constitution were ignored because, according to Davies, "constitutions and civil liberties in eastern Europe were regarded as a dangerous disease, and the Poles were suspected of being the main carriers of contagion."[16] The Russian czars, facing peasant revolts in their own country, were suspicious of Poles because they feared Poles might give Russians ideas about resisting tyranny. Hostile toward the Congress Kingdom from the beginning, Russia was simply waiting for an excuse to destroy it.

RESISTANCE AND PUNISHMENT

That chance came with the November Rising of 1830. Nicholas I, czar of Russia since 1825, was not temperamentally suited to be anything other than a dictatorial ruler, and he hated even the vestiges of independence exercised by the Congress Kingdom—its parliament, army, administration, and schools. Nicholas used a Polish rebellion in the aftermath of an assassination attempt on his brother as an excuse to invade the Congress Kingdom. After a short war, the Polish forces were defeated and a few years later the Congress Kingdom became the Russian province of Vistulaland, with no separate constitution or government. Elsewhere, in 1846 an insurrection in Kraków led to its reabsorption into Galicia, and thus by midcentury the partitions were fully back in place.

Russian troops occupy Warsaw shortly after the November Rising of 1830. Russian czar Nicholas I put down the Polish rebellion and exiled 80,000 people to Siberia.

GRANDMOTHER'S RING

Ola Szczerbińska, who grew up to marry Józef Pilsudski, one of the heroes of the partition era and later years, recounted in her memoirs a conversation she had when she was seven years old with her grandmother, a former gun-runner and spy. Szczerbińska later said this conversation, reprinted in Norman Davies's *Heart of Europe: A Short History of Poland*, made her want nothing more than to grow up to be a revolutionary herself.

My grandmother was a woman of great intelligence and strength of character. . . . Patriotism was the main motor of her life . . . and in the conspiratorial work of the January Rising [1863] she had played a prominent part. . . . The Rising's failure caused the greatest trauma of her life. Henceforward, she always wore the same black dress, and on her finger a ring decorated with a white cross in pearls on black enamel.

—It's a ring of mourning for those who died, she said.

But when I asked to put it on my finger, she shook her head.

—You can only wear it when you're a real patriot. . . .

—And what does that mean, Grandma, "being a patriot"?

—A patriot is someone who loves Poland above everything else in the world, and will abandon everything, even life itself, for her Freedom. . . .

—I want to fight for Poland, Grandma, I said, only half comprehending.

After a while my grandmother's eyes flashed.

—Yes. . . . Do you promise to fight for Poland, my child?

—I promise, Grandma. I repeated, enthralled by the ominous feeling.

Then she caressed me, and placing the ring on my finger, held it there tightly.

—Now there, run along. . . . But don't forget, and don't tell a soul.

Those who resisted the Russians expected to pay a high price for doing so. After the November Rising, for example, eighty thousand rebels and family members were sent across Russia to Siberia, in central Asia, many of them walking in chains for long distances to rail depots where they were crammed into cattle cars for the rest of the journey. The point of such exile was not to have all the prisoners actually arrive and complete their sentences, but to kill most of them slowly through the hardships of the journey, and then to work the survivors to death. By and large the inhumane strategy worked. Accurate records were not kept and the total number of those who died, or even how many survived will never be known, although in Siberia today there are families of Polish descent whose ancestors came as prisoners.

Resistance, regardless of which partitioning power it was directed against, took many less obvious forms than participating in open rebellions. However, according to Davies,

> the authorities made no distinction between different degrees of resistance, nor between the different methods employed. There was no appreciation of a "legal opposition," let alone of "non-violent" resistance. There was no chance of working openly within the law by some glib, public rejection of one's private sympathies for terrorist colleagues; there was no opportunity for stating one's case in public.[17]

In short, the Poles came to expect to suffer or die for even the slightest shows of lack of enthusiasm for their oppression. But still they resisted, and created both stubbornness of character and willingness to die for seemingly hopeless causes that is still remarked upon by historians and social scientists today. In the words of Davies,

> over the generations they produced a crowded gallery of adventurers, folk heroes, and martyrs. They were men and women, careless of their own safety, who fought against tyranny wherever it was found. . . . In the eyes of some of their . . . compatriots, they were dangerous, suicidal fanatics, and to the authorities, simple terrorists. Yet not even their enemies could deny that they were often people of principle, moved by deep moral convictions.[18]

EMILIA PLATER

Patriotism and a willingness to die for Poland were not strictly masculine traits. In fact, according to Norman Davies in *Heart of Europe: A Short History of Poland,* "if the typical Polish 'patriot' at any time up to 1864 had been a young man with a sabre or revolver in his hand, the typical patriot at the turn of the century was a young lady of good family with a textbook under her shawl."

Many young women, unable to leave home to fight, still risked their lives to educate people about Polish culture and revolutionary ideas. Others, however, did take sabre or revolver in hand. One of these was Emilia Plater, a Lithuanian by birth. Plater disguised herself as a man and raised a band of local peasants to fight in Lithuania in one of the nearly innumerable uprisings that characterized the era. She later became an infantry captain, and fought in three battles with the Russians. While leading troops trying to break through to capture Warsaw, she stopped for the night in a peasant's cottage and was found dead in the morning, apparently a victim of complete exhaustion. She was twenty-five. Poet Adam Mickiewicz described the death scene in a flowery poem titled in English "The Death of the Colonel":

> But look! This soldier, though dressed in soldier's clothes,
> Has the fairest face of a maiden, and a woman's
> Gentle breast. These mortal remains
> Are those of the rebel leader, the virgin-martyr,
> The girl from Lithuania—Emilia Plater!

CULTURE WARS AND THE CATHOLIC CHURCH

A little later in the nineteenth century, in the Prussian partition, Poles were mounting a different, though still dangerous, kind of resistance to Prince Otto von Bismarck's Kulturkampf. The Kulturkampf, or "culture war," was an attempt beginning in 1872 by the northern Protestant Germans to eradicate the southern Catholic German culture. For many years the southern Germans had dominated political life, and Bismarck was determined to change that forever.

Otto von Bismarck launched his Kulturkampf to suppress Catholicism in southern Germany and Poland.

The cornerstone of the Kulturkampf was suppression of the Catholic faith and Catholic institutions such as the churches and the clergy. Though it was really directed toward Germans, the net result was to further alienate the staunchly Catholic Poles, who turned to the church for help in resisting the hated Germans. According to writers Mark Salter and Gordon McLachlan, the Kulturkampf "misfired badly in Poland, giving the clergy the opportunity to whip up support for their own fervently nationalistic brand of Catholicism."[19]

The church had always been a major element in Polish life since Mieszko's conversion almost one thousand years before, but during the partitions it became associated with the cause of liberation from oppression. Many resistance leaders came from within the clergy. In addition to producing some individual priests of great courage, the Catholic Church was important during the partitions in another way as well. Based outside of Poland, in Rome, the church was able to take positions against the oppression in Poland without fear of suffering the same consequences people within Poland would face. Thus it became one of the forces keeping the plight of the Poles from being ignored by the rest of Europe. This feeling of not being forgotten was one of the things enabling the Poles to keep their hopes for liberation and reunification alive through generation after generation of partition.

For all the good the Catholic Church did in keeping the Poles' morale high, Catholic nationalism began to take some ominous turns late in the nineteenth century. In the Prussian partition, where ethnic and religious differences were already being fanned into resentment and hatred because of

An old Catholic church in southern Poland. The church gave people hope during the partition years, bringing their plight to the attention of the rest of Europe.

HOW POLISH JEWS GOT THEIR LAST NAMES

During the partitions Jews, who traditionally had not had surnames, were required to go to the Prussian registry to receive one. In Warsaw the registry was run by E. T. A. Hoffmann, the same man who wrote the stories on which Jacques Offenbach based his opera *Tales of Hoffmann*. His flippant treatment of the applicants for surnames may be extreme, but nevertheless reflects the general disrespect of the Prussians for the Poles— Jewish or otherwise. One contemporary account, quoted by Norman Davies in *Heart of Europe: A Short History of Poland*, describes how Hoffman chose the names.

"He has a long, stringy neck, wrapped in a Turkish scarf, and a large head of tangled hair. He glares at the client in deathly silence, and then shouts out the first word that comes to mind. This word, which the clerk enters into the Register, becomes the client's official surname." One day he had fish for dinner, and afterward named everyone after fishes, and another day he received a bouquet of roses and gave everyone rose names. "On another occasion, having visited the district of Warsaw where cage-birds are sold, he came back to the office and created a mass of VOGELS [birds]. Once when Hoffman had been playing the organ in church, he issued a string of surnames with a religious flavour, such as HELFGOT, HIMMELBLAU . . . and so on." After a night of drinking with a Prussian colonel he came in with a hangover and asked to have cold water poured over his head, after which he started issuing military sounding surnames. The eyewitness account concludes, "That's as far as he got, because the rest of his clients fled."

the Kulturkampf, the idea began to take hold that one could not be a true Pole without also being Catholic. As Polishness and Catholicism began to merge, anti-Semitism gained strength, spelling the end of a five-hundred-year history of tolerance and paving the way for Jewish extermination in the Holocaust in the next century.

THE ÉMIGRÉS

The Catholic Church was not the only force outside Poland working to keep a sense of nationhood alive in an era when, according to Davies, "notes, protests, and rejoinders about

Poland fell thick as autumn leaves."[20] Perhaps the single most powerful element of protest was the Polish émigré. Leaving Poland for economic and other reasons, émigrés settled in western Europe or America in cities such as Chicago, which still has a large Polish American community today. Their memories of their native land enabled them to ignite international sympathy for the plight of the Poles who remained behind.

Others left for political reasons, concluding that life would be impossible for them in partitioned Poland. Many felt this way because their identity was so wrapped up in being Polish that they could not have expressed themselves at all without being persecuted for it. Perhaps the most famous of these émigrés was pianist and composer Frédéric Chopin, who moved to France to be free to compose as he wished. Chopin's music, based on Polish folk melodies and energetic dances such as the mazurka and the "polonaise" (whose name means "in the Polish style"), took France by storm.

Composer Frédéric Chopin emigrated from Poland but carried Polish culture with him, basing much of his music on traditional folk tunes.

Chopin serves as a good example of the curious fact that Polish cultural greatness likely survived in the nineteenth century only because so many great Poles left. Strange as it may seem, the only people called Poles were the ones who lived abroad because those who stayed home were called by the name of their partitioning power. At home, for example, Chopin would have been called a Russian. Whether they were consciously political or not, émigrés such as Chopin, physicist Marie Curie, actress Helena Modjeska, pianist Ignacy Paderewski, poet Guillaume Apollinaire, novelist Joseph Conrad, and anthropologist Bronislaw Malinowski were the clearest expressions of Polish identity, intellect, and spirit in the nineteenth century.

Though some Polish émigrés simply wanted room to pursue their scientific or artistic interests, many others ceaselessly tried to reestablish Poland as a free nation. Some Polish émigrés, centered in the Hotel Lambert in Paris, lived relatively quiet lives writing articles for publication in sympathetic newspapers and journals. Others modeled themselves after the popular image of the swashbuckling, romantic hero willing to die for a noble cause, and they launched one failed military campaign after another all over Europe to weaken the stranglehold of the partitioning powers.

Some Polish patriots, including Adam Mickiewicz, were a combination of the two types. Mickiewicz was one of Poland's greatest poets, but he was torn between his desire to write and the urge to act on behalf of his beloved country. His life story is full of the kinds of activities that were typical of Polish émigrés of his time. In 1823, when he was twenty-five, Mickiewicz was exiled from Poland to Russia for five years for being part of a Polish patriotic society. He was never permitted to return to Poland and spent the rest of his life wandering from place to place trying to stir up revolts against the partitions. After some time in France, he made his way to Italy, where he organized a legion to fight against Austria, one of the partitioning powers. He stayed on to fight in several small uprisings in Italy and later organized a regiment of Jews to fight against Russia, another partitioning power. He was organizing yet another legion when he died of cholera at age forty-five. In the time between all these activities he managed to write what is considered Poland's finest epic poem, *Dziady* (1832), in which he depicts Poland as Christlike, scourged and oppressed but ultimately able to rise again. He also wrote another epic poem, *Pan Tadeusz* (1834), which evokes an idyllic version of Polish life before the partitions. Mickiewicz's life and works illustrate how the émigrés' love of country came to consume their whole lives.

World War I

According to writers Mark Salter and Gordon McLachlan, "World War I smashed the might of the Russian, German, and Austrian empires and allowed Poland to rise from the dead."[21] Sadly, before this resurrection could occur, Poles who had been told they were Russians had to fight against Poles who had been told they were Germans, killing each other in battles that destroyed the Polish countryside. Morale among Poles was at its lowest point, because they were watching their land and people be ruined in the name of the nations who had spent the last century trying to destroy them.

To gain support among Poles for a war which was being fought in part on Polish soil and which was killing so many Poles, Great Britain vowed that Poland would become an independent country after the war. For over a century Poles had been trying to get this kind of support. Thus, the deaths of thousands of Polish soldiers who fought alongside the British in the Allied army, and the suffering of millions more at home, created a situation after the war where Great Britain could not even think about going back on that promise. It did not renege, nor did it want to. Thus, in the ashes of a broken continent, Poland was brought back to life by the Allied victory over Germany. The partitions were over and the name of Poland could once again be proudly on the lips of its citizens as well as in their hearts and minds.

4

Between Two Tyrants: Poland Under the Nazis and Communists

Poland was resurrected as a nation in 1918, but it faced many immediate problems, ranging from the relatively simple, like creating a new currency, to the staggeringly complex, like restructuring the Prussian, Austrian, and Russian legal systems into a single Polish one. Though these challenges would be daunting enough, several other problems quickly arose which would shape Poland in the decades to come. The first of these was ethnicity. At the end of the partitions more than a quarter of the people who lived within Poland's borders were ethnic minorities—Lithuanians, Belarusians, Germans, Czechs, Ukrainians, and Jews. To some this meant that a quarter of the people in Poland were foreigners even though their families might have been there for generations. To others "Pole" was not an ethnic distinction, but a matter of citizenship. To them, every one of Poland's citizens was a "Pole." As the century progressed, the non-ethnic Poles, particularly Jews, would come to see how strong many people's feelings were about whether non-ethnic Poles belonged in Poland at all.

A second factor keeping Poland from emerging as a strong, united country in the early twentieth century was the range of opinions about what kind of government and society the Poles wanted to have. But while Poles were busy with internal politics, the nations around them were once again drifting toward war. World War II broke out in 1939, followed by almost four decades of forced communist rule in Poland. Not until near the end of the century would Poles have the chance again to have a say in how their country would be run.

JÓZEF PILSUDSKI AND ROMAN DMOWSKI

The disagreements between the two major political figures of the period between the wars, Józef Pilsudski and Roman Dmowski, illustrate the divisiveness in the nation. Pilsudski, who often fought on horseback with a sword, emerged from World War I as a legendary hero. Pilsudski was convinced that the only way for Poland to survive between Germany and Russia was to develop as a great military power itself. He advocated a large, strong army, and a society in which military officers were considered the elite. Watching with alarm the newly formed Soviet Union's desire to gain more power in the west, Pilsudski also favored a federation with other border nations to ward off possible Soviet invasion. He also believed strongly in a Poland which saw all of its citizens as Poles.

General Józef Pilsudski reviews a battalion of Polish infantry. Pilsudski, dictator of Poland from 1926 to 1935, wanted his country to become a strong military power.

Roman Dmowski, head of the Nationalist League party and opponent of Pilsudski.

Pilsudski's views about the military elite were not popular with a nation that disliked the idea of a powerful upper class, but his military leadership was wanted in a nation uneasy about the powerful, well-armed countries surrounding it. Pilsudski refused to run in Poland's first presidential election in 1922 because he felt the office of president did not have enough real power. However, by 1926 he had decided that his approach was essential to the nation's survival and staged a military takeover. Calling his new government Sanacja, from the Polish word for sanitation, Pilsudski remained Poland's self-appointed president until his death in 1935, overseeing an increasingly authoritarian government which many felt was the key to keeping Poland alive and healthy.

In contrast, Roman Dmowski, leader of another party called the Nationalist League, wanted the average Polish citizen to be the most powerful element in Polish society. Dmowski's power base was among the many farmers and other rural residents of Poland. Staunchly Catholic, they wanted Roman Catholicism to be the official, or even only, faith in Poland. Thus, supporters of Dmowski's Nationalist League thought that the best thing for Poland would be if each ethnic group had its own territory within Poland, or better yet, left Poland altogether. The goal was a Poland run exclusively by and for ethnic Poles. Dmowski was never able to unseat Pilsudski, although his version of what at the end of the twentieth century is commonly called "ethnic cleansing" gained popularity during the 1920s and 1930s.

ECONOMIC TROUBLES AND THE RISE OF ANTI-SEMITISM

Some of Dmowski's popularity came about as a result of economic problems in Poland which many blamed on others in their midst, particularly the Jews. The vast majority of Jews were small shopkeepers or self-employed in skilled trades, and they had no more economic power than the average non-Jew, but still anti-Semites felt that Jews were somehow responsible for all economic problems in Poland and abroad. The economic problems were real, but in Poland the true causes included the fact that many of the industries and larger businesses in Poland were owned not by Poles but by citizens of the partitioning powers. Thus, even successful businesses did not do much to build Poland's economy because the profits were sent abroad to their owners. The economic picture was also bleak in rural areas, where farms were grossly inefficient due to their small size and lack of machinery.

WORLD WAR II

As the 1930s came to a close, the Polish mood became even more subdued. In 1937, Nazi leader Adolf Hitler annexed Austria and in 1938, he occupied the Sudetenland, a part of the Czech Republic right on the Polish border. Though Poland was sure that the Allies would come to its defense if it were invaded, the prospect of a war to defend Polish soil raised horrible memories of the recent death and destruction during World War I. Then, on September 1, 1939, the Polish people's worst fear was realized: Hitler's army invaded Poland and World War II was declared. The Poles were caught by surprise by the sudden massive invasion of tanks and soldiers, and by October the nation had fallen.

Shortly before the invasion, the Soviet Union and Germany had signed a secret Nazi-Soviet Non-Aggression Pact, which established that neither would move to stop the other's aggression in Europe and contained a secret agreement to divide Poland between them. As soon as the treaty was signed, Hitler invaded Poland, and within two weeks Russia had invaded from the east up to the agreed-upon division line. Poland was thus fighting on two fronts, as Soviet leader Joseph Stalin moved his army west to gain territory in eastern Poland. According to Waldemar Paclawski and Alfred Horn, "[t]here were cases of Polish soldiers caught in the middle of this crushing onslaught, who fought the Germans in the morning and Soviet forces on the afternoon of the same day."[22] Once the Soviets and Germans had claimed their Polish "entitlement," they signed a treaty and moved on to other conquests, leaving in their wake an occupied Poland which over the next four years would suffer as much or more than any country in Europe, losing 6 million of its citizens, including almost all its Jewish citizens, as well as 40 percent of its buildings.

OSKAR SCHINDLER

Oskar Schindler, made famous by Thomas Keneally's 1982 book, *Schindler's List,* and Steven Spielberg's Oscar-winning 1993 movie of the same name, was born to a German family in 1908 in the Sudetenland area of Czechoslovakia, near the Polish border. He moved to Poland in 1930, and when Poland fell to the Nazis he saw a chance to profit from forced Jewish labor. He bought a bankrupt enamelware factory in Kraków and refitted it to produce munitions. At the beginning he was thinking only of himself, but as the situation of the Jews worsened, he began to understand that he could save them by keeping them employed in an industry essential to the war effort. When the Kraków ghetto was liquidated and the Jews were sent to Auschwitz or labor camps such as Plaszów, outside Kraków, Schindler succeeded in keeping twelve hundred of them from certain death.

After the war, Schindler moved to Argentina with his wife Emilie and his mistress. He tried other businesses but they all failed. It seemed he was right, as his character in the movie *Schindler's List* stated: The difference between success and failure for him was the existence of a war. When he became so poor he faced debtor's prison, the Jews he had saved sent him money and continued to support him. Their appreciation for him was so strong that he visited them at their expense in Israel each year; when he died in 1974 his body was buried in Jerusalem.

No one has quite satisfactorily explained why Schindler had the turnabout that caused him to risk his life to save the Schindlerjuden, or Schindler Jews, as they called themselves. He was unable to explain it himself, and many people feel he is one example of many—unfortunately not enough—ordinary people who briefly became more than it seemed they could be when the situation required it.

Oskar Schindler gives a speech at a gathering in Israel to honor his assistance to Jews during the Holocaust.

JEWISH GHETTOS AND THE FINAL SOLUTION

Regardless of their ancestry, Poles found themselves targets of the Nazis. Slavs were considered by the Nazis to be sub-human, and Jews were considered to be even below Slavs. Early in the war, many Poles were uprooted from their homes so Germans could move into their communities. Those of value to the war effort were sent to forced labor camps, and the rest were deported to other parts of Poland. Those who resisted or were seen as security risks were shot or sent to camps where most were murdered, or starved and worked to death.

But it was the Jews who were prime targets of the Nazi terror. According to Israel Gutman, historian of the Holocaust,

> Jews were first . . . required to wear the Jewish star. Jewish property was confiscated and the remaining Jewish shops were marked. From local shops to art collections, from factories to private libraries, the Nazis followed a disciplined procedure of confiscation. All radios were

THE JUDENRAT

During World War II the Jewish ghettos were run by a council of Jewish residents, the Judenrat, which reported to the Nazis. The role of the Judenrat is still a subject of debate today: Did its leaders betray the Jews and assist in their destruction or did they provide the only possible buffer between ghetto residents and the Nazis and thus keep more Jews alive, in hope of eventual liberation? For example, once ordered to wear Stars of David to identify themselves as Jews, and forced to live in the ghetto, it was easy for Nazis to roam the streets kidnapping large numbers of people for forced labor. Many residents never returned. Daily kidnappings stopped when the Judenrat agreed to provide a certain number of forced laborers every day. The Judenrat itself enforced every new Nazi edict such as taxes and bans so that the increasingly vicious Nazi soldiers would have no need to enter the ghetto.

Their dual role as both betrayer and savior was evidenced by the 1942 suicide of the leader of the Warsaw Judenrat, Adam Czerniakow. His special passion was for keeping orphaned children from being sent to Auschwitz, though he was vilified by many Jews for otherwise cooperating with the Nazis. When he was finally told to produce the children for deportation, he took cyanide rather than do so. According to Israel Gutman in *Resistance: The Warsaw Ghetto Uprising*, Czerniakow left behind a note saying "the SS wants me to kill children with my own hands." Even after his death he was criticized for lacking the courage to stand up to the Nazis, but others saw him simply as a man broken by the moral quandaries he had faced.

taken. Collective responsibility and punishment were imposed: the deed of one endangered all. Jews were isolated from their former neighbors and concentrated into restricted living quarters.[23]

These living quarters were known as the Jewish ghettos.

For the Nazis, ridding Poland of its Jews seemed to be possible by cramming them all into a few blocks and sealing them in with a brick wall, thus leaving them to die of starvation and diseases. What happened in Warsaw in 1940 was typical of all Polish cities. Four percent of Warsaw was designated for Jews, who represented 30 percent of the population. The problem was aggravated when Jews from the surrounding countryside were forced there as well. The ghetto population swelled to almost a half million in a few square block radius, before people started dying in massive numbers. Warsaw ghetto residents were given food totaling only 184 calories a day on which to live. A thriving black market and smuggled goods kept them alive.

What was euphemistically called the Final Solution went into operation sometime around the beginning of 1941, to speed up the process of eliminating the Jews. Outside most large Polish cities, camps with gas chambers and crematoria were built to handle mass executions. By 1942, the ghettos began to be cleared of their residents, who were sent in systematic waves, beginning with the least fit and the least useful, to die by the millions in camps such as Auschwitz, Majdanek, and Treblinka.

POLAND UNDER STALIN

Although the Final Solution was specifically a Nazi undertaking, Jews and all other Poles in the area occupied by the Soviet Union suffered dramatically as well. Stalin believed that the spirit of the Polish people had to be broken before Poland could be successfully brought under the control of the Soviet Union. Essential to his plan was massive deportation of Poles to break their ties to their land. In just one year, over 1.5 million Poles were deported farther east in Poland or to the Soviet Union. Many went to concentration camps for forced labor and "reeducation" into Soviet ways. Though these camps were not officially "death camps" set up for the sole purpose of killing people, by 1942 they had nevertheless resulted in the death of half of their residents. Life outside the camps was not much safer. For example, in 1943 a grave holding the remains of forty-five hundred Polish army officers was uncovered at Katyn, but Poland is full of similar mass graves.

German soldiers laugh as they watch a Polish Orthodox Jew say a prayer for executed Jews in Poland in 1939.

THE WARSAW GHETTO UPRISING

The question is often asked: Why did the Jews not fight harder for their lives? Why did so few see the Holocaust coming and escape while there was still time? Answers are hotly debated and as complex as human beings themselves. But what is often forgotten is that Jews did not always go peaceably into the cattle cars headed for Auschwitz, or willingly dig the graves into which a bullet to the head would make them fall. Jews did rise up, even against hopeless odds, as the 1943 Warsaw Ghetto Uprising illustrates.

By 1942 conditions in the ghetto had taken their intended toll, and one-quarter of the residents had died. But by this point the nearby death camp at Treblinka was ready, and mass deportations could begin. The Nazis began clearing the ghetto, taking three hundred thousand of its residents that summer. Devastated by the fact that they had not fought back sooner, the sixty thousand remaining ghetto residents, mostly young men and women still strong enough to work, resolved to fight to keep the Nazis from entering the ghetto. Leaders of the Jewish Combat Organization (ZOB) led the effort. From then on, every time Nazi soldiers came through the gates they were forced back by homemade bombs, smuggled guns, rocks, and whatever else was at hand.

Finally, in April 1943, the Nazis launched a full-scale assault on the ghetto. Despite their overwhelming military superiority and successful espionage campaign, they were unable to capture the rebels or find their headquarters for almost a month. When they finally entered the ZOB's bunker, they found ZOB leader Mordechai Anieliewicz and the leading ZOB members dead in a suicide pact. Over the next few weeks, the Nazis roamed the ghetto looking for anyone still alive, burning and bombing the ghetto to the ground, to kill those in hiding or force them out so they could shoot them or send them to the death camps. A few people escaped or were rescued by heroic outsiders who risked death to enter to rescue them, but almost to the last of their numbers they died.

According to historian Israel Gutman, in *Resistance: The Warsaw Ghetto Uprising,* "if victory eluded them, honor and dignity did not. One thousand years of Jewish heritage had come to an end in Poland not with a whimper or with the cries of cowering masses, but with the courageous acts of young fighters who stood to defend their honor—who resisted despite the overwhelming power of the foe."

POLISH RESISTANCE

From the beginning the Polish people resisted the Nazi and Soviet armies. In the words of British prime minister Winston Churchill, "Poland was the only occupied country which never collaborated with the Nazis in any form. . . . To the Nazi terror Poland replied with a mass resistance movement, one of the strongest in Europe."[24] Resistance took a number of forms. With the financial support of the Allies, approximately 350,000 soldiers were organized into the Armia Krajowa (AK) or Home Army, which reported to the London-based Polish government-in-exile of Wladyslaw Sikorski, and fought wherever they were sent as part of the Allied forces. Some who remained in occupied Poland became spies and saboteurs. Many risked—and some lost—their lives in efforts to keep Jews alive in the ghettos by smuggling food, or by providing safe hiding places outside the ghettos. Others, including many teenage girls and boys, served as runners, slipping across Poland to tell the Jews of one city about the situation of Jews in another, to inform Polish resistance fighters about troop or supply movements, and to get information to the outside world about atrocities taking place in Poland.

Late in the war, resistance took another form when the Nazis began retreating from Poland. By this time Hitler had made a disastrous attempt to invade Russia; the Soviet Union had broken its alliance with the Nazis and joined the Allied forces. The Soviet Union chased the Nazis off Polish soil and officially liberated Polish cities by establishing military control and an interim government. However, Stalin's mistreatment of the Polish people had made this not seem like liberation at all, and the Poles feared—rightly, it turned out—that if the Communists ever took the Polish capital, they would not willingly relinquish control. Thus, it seemed essential for Poles to liberate Warsaw themselves. If they could reestablish Poland as an independent country by this symbolic gesture, there would be no need for the Soviets even to enter the city.

The Warsaw Uprising, as the Polish attempt to liberate Warsaw is known, lasted for sixty-three days in the autumn of 1944. Because the Soviets wanted to "liberate" Warsaw themselves and thus be able to set up a communist government, they wanted the uprising to fail. To ensure this, the

Soviets would not permit Allied supply convoys to cross any territory they had "liberated," nor let planes carrying provisions in support of the uprising refuel. Thus, Warsaw was isolated, and the Nazis still in the city were able to crush the uprising. Poles still harbor bitterness today toward the Russians because at the time of the uprising, the Soviet army simply waited across the Vistula River in the suburb of Praga, within sight of the destruction, and did nothing to stop it. Once the rebellion was crushed, the Nazis began retreating. In revenge for the uprising, on Hitler's orders, the German army left behind only a pile of rubble where the city had once stood. Then the Russians simply crossed the Vistula and "liberated" Warsaw.

THE AFTERMATH OF WAR

By the end of the war, Poland had lost millions of citizens. Whole cities were in ruins, as were the railroads and industries needed for recovery. On top of these problems, by the

COMMUNISM

In eastern Europe and Russia, communism began its rise in the 1910s and had fallen by the 1990s. The philosophy of communism is based in the idea that when humans have individual and personal gain as their goal, one person generally succeeds at the expense of another. Over time a society evolves in which the rich and successful are unconcerned about anyone but themselves. Most people stay poor despite hard work, while the people who own their workplaces grow richer. In contrast, if workers collectively owned farms and factories, Communists argue, the fruit of their labor could be fairly shared and quality of life would improve. The basic idea was that everyone would work as hard as possible and then have all their needs met by the profits of everyone's combined labor. No one would be rich or poor, and everyone would be housed, clothed, and fed.

The idea behind communism was immensely popular in the late nineteenth and early twentieth centuries, especially in countries where nobles lived off the labor of workers on their estates. It also was popular in large cities, where the poor worked long hours in appalling conditions in factories when they earned too little to feed their families. But, though governments based on communist ideals took hold around the world in the twentieth century, by century's end in Europe they were almost all gone. There are many theories about why they failed, but the simplest seems to be human nature.

Most people have noticed that staying motivated to work hard for no reward is difficult. In many communist countries, people working on collective farms or in state-owned factories did not want to work any harder than the next person, because the extra work would earn them nothing. Productivity on farming collectives dropped so low that food shortages became critical. Factories produced less and the quality of goods declined. Force and terrorism became necessary to keep a communist system in place when people ceased to believe that it could really make their lives better.

Also, despite the fact that no one was supposed to get ahead at anyone else's expense under the communist system, chances for personal gain were irresistible to many communist leaders. The ideals of communism were undercut by the fact that many party leaders lived like the nobility of old, while others went hungry. This undermined their credibility, and caused more resentment. Thus, in the end communism failed in Europe because it could not deliver on the promise of a better life.

time the peace conference at Yalta established spheres of power in postwar Europe, Stalin's troops had advanced all the way across Poland and had already set up Stalin's appointed leaders at the head of a communist government.

Thus, at the conference, Poland was recognized as an independent nation, but Stalin was not forced to withdraw. By these tactics Poland fell into communist hands, and would spend the next forty years behind what soon became known as the iron curtain.

POLAND UNDER COMMUNISM

The Poles made reluctant Communists. In the 1946 elections, the majority of Poles voted to replace Stalin's government with a democratic government headed by Stanislaw Mikolajczyk, who had been head of the government-in-exile at the end of the war. Mikolajczyk won the election easily, but somehow the results were manipulated so that the overwhelming majority of the seats in the Sejm went to the communist-ruled Democratic Block, which immediately held its own election and installed Boleslaw Bierut as president.

Under Bierut, repressive Stalin-style communism took hold, with disastrous early results. A huge army was assembled to protect against what people were told was the threat of invasion by people from western countries, an army that was ruthlessly turned against anyone who protested against the government. Poland was told it needed to produce steel, coal, and armaments to help the Soviets defend communism against supposed threats from western countries, but it did not have much of the machinery it would need; what it did have had been dismantled and taken to Russia. The communist government said it would provide all the food people needed and it outlawed private stores. Government stores were to be supplied by huge government farms called collectives, which the Communists said would be superior to Poland's individually owned small farms. When the state could not keep the stores adequately supplied, people had to wait in long lines for the few available items, and many were so poorly fed that Poland was brought to the brink of starvation.

Stalin's promises of vastly improved lives quickly faded, as communism failed to rebuild the economy. The huge army made any sign of dissent an excuse for a bloodbath. Change through elections was ruled out by the fact that the only permissible political groups were those controlled by the Communists, called in Poland the Polish United Workers' Party, or PZPR. Thus, despite the wishes of the majority of its citizens, Poland remained in the hands of a Stalin-controlled government.

Bread and Liberty

By the early 1950s, dissent simmered close to the surface. The Catholic Church once again became one of the leading forces of opposition, and as a result saw its assets confiscated by the Communists and its priests harassed and frequently banished. Another dissenting voice, Wladyslaw Gomulka, leader of the Polish Communists and sworn enemy of Stalin's repressive leadership, quickly found himself in prison.

When Stalin died in 1953, the effect on Poland was evident. Gomulka was released in 1954 and became party chief—effectively the leader of Poland. Poland, though remaining Communist, was determined to chart its own course: the proof was that Gomulka was elected without consulting Nikita Khrushchev, the new leader of the Soviet Union. This angered Khrushchev, and it appeared for a while that the Soviets might invade Poland as they had Hungary to put down what were perceived as treasonous shows of independence. Only Gomulka's assurances of his commitment to communism and Poland's desire to remain allied with the Soviet Union kept Poland from being swallowed up. Thus, under Gomulka a Polish-style communism was able to evolve. Gomulka's move allowed churches that had been suppressed by the Communists to reopen, saved small farms from collectivization, and permitted at least some freedom of speech.

Wladyslaw Gomulka became the Polish communist party chief in 1954.

But a modified form of communism proved scarcely more popular with the average Pole. The economy did not recover. There were still only communist political candidates to vote for. People were starving. Neither Gomulka nor Edward Gierek, who succeeded him as party leader in 1970, had any true support among the masses. As dissatisfaction grew in the 1960s and 1970s, the communist leadership resorted to force and curtailment of freedoms such as the ability to hold protest marches. Every few years protests broke out anyway, led by students, workers, and intellectuals waving banners proclaiming "Bread and Liberty." Each time the revolts were put down by force, the bitterness of Poles toward their government grew.

SOLIDARITY

In 1980, nationwide strikes broke out when the government attempted to impose a major increase in the price of food. The strike began in the Lenin shipyard in Gdańsk, and a thirty-seven-year-old worker, Lech Wałęsa, emerged as its leader. The strikers had a number of demands, including the right to strike legally without government retaliation, the right to form independent unions, and the right to build a memorial for shipyard workers killed in a strike a decade before. According to historian Timothy Garton Ash, Wałęsa's charisma was obvious from the start. When the government refused to permit construction of a memorial, Wałęsa said "everyone should come back next

The 1980 strikes at the Lenin shipyard in Gdańsk that ignited the Solidarity movement continued on through the decade. Here, crowds of strikers gather at the main gate of the Lenin shipyard in 1988.

JERZY POPIELUSZKO

Toward the end of communist rule in Poland, when the government was trying to suppress Solidarity, many Catholic clergy came to the forefront to fight for free speech and reform. One of these priests was Jerzy Popieluszko, who was the spiritual adviser for the Solidarity movement. His fiery sermons and other activities in defiance of the government made him a target for retaliation, and in 1984 he was murdered by members of the government's security police.

Father Popieluszko's death spurred outrage by the church and public alike. After a public trial, through which the involvement of Wojciech Jaruzelski's government in the murder was made clear, the security service was forced to reorganize and its power was curtailed. Approximately 70 percent of its personnel were let go, and two departments which had monitored such things as the press, social organizations, and the church were abolished altogether in an attempt to placate the Polish people.

In return, the Jaruzelski regime demanded that the church limit itself to nonpolitical activities and punish dissident clergy itself. The usually docile church hierarchy, encouraged by the fact that the sitting pope, John Paul II, was strongly opposed to Polish communism, responded by demanding greater guarantees of free speech and assembly as well as the release of political prisoners. Jaruzelski gave in and offered amnesty to five hundred prisoners.

When the pope visited Poland in 1986, he met with Jaruzelski in a symbolic gesture of reconciliation. On a visit to Poland in 1988, Great Britain's prime minister, Margaret Thatcher, visited Popieluszko's grave. This served as a reminder to Jaruzelski that the Western world was aware that, despite some rather showy attempts at reform, dissidents were still being harassed and the struggle for human rights was far from won.

year, same place, same time . . . and each carrying a stone. If the authorities refused to build a monument, they would build it themselves!"[25] The movement Wałęsa led began calling itself Solidarność, or Solidarity.

Fearing that if a year passed, there would be a pile of stones a mile high at the Lenin shipyard, the government agreed to meet with Solidarity leaders. Wałęsa and others clarified that they did not want to overthrow communism, but simply wanted their needs recognized and addressed. The government agreed to these demands, and also agreed to recognize Solidarity as a legal and official group—the first recognized union in communist Poland. Within a few months a Farmers' Solidarity was also formed. The overall Solidarity movement soon had 10 million members.

But what seemed to most Poles as a major step forward was short lived. In a little over a year, the Communist Party–appointed leader of Poland, General Wojciech Jaruzelski, declared martial law, disbanded the movement, and imprisoned many of its leaders. This was not simply because he feared the union's growing popularity but because the Soviet Union had made it clear that they were prepared to invade Poland to restore order if Jaruzelski could not do it himself. Jaruzelski felt that a crackdown on Solidarity and any other dissent was the only way to keep Poland's even partial independence. But the Poles were no longer willing to submit to harsh rule. The world treated their leaders with respect—Lech Walęsa received the Nobel Peace Prize in 1983 and Archbishop Karol Wojtyla, an outspoken opponent of communism, had become Pope John Paul II in 1978—and it was only in their own country, at the hands of their own countrymen, that they felt disrespected.

For the next few years, Poles simply disregarded their government. In the words of Paclawski and Horn, "[l]ife was divided into two spheres—the official legal, everyday routine and the unofficial, illegal, underground work."[26] The economy was in collapse; when the black market became the way most people managed to get what they needed to survive, it became clear that the government could not take care of the people at all. In a desperate attempt to pull Poland back on track, Jaruzelski called for a referendum in which people could vote yes or no on his plan to increase food prices in exchange for a promise of establishing democracy. The people voted it down; according to Salter and McLachlan, "the real message of the vote [was] a rejection not merely of the [program] but of the notion that the Party could lead Poland out of its crisis."[27] Massive strikes followed the referendum, and Jaruzelski was finally forced to acknowledge that the party would have to share power with Solidarity.

A series of talks in 1989 resulted in agreements centering around the right to form unions and political parties, establishment of a free press, and the promise of open elections. The Polish people resoundingly defeated the Communists in a quickly called 1989 parliamentary election, and in 1990 Lech Walęsa was elected president of Poland. Finally, after nearly two centuries of almost uninterrupted oppression, the Poles had chosen how and by whom they would be led.

AFTER COMMUNISM: POLAND TODAY

At the end of the twentieth century Poles would discover what earlier generations had discovered at its beginning: It is easier to dream of freedom than to make it work. As in countries all across eastern Europe, Soviet dominance had provided some kind of structure, although a widely disliked one. Left to govern themselves, Poles quickly found that wounds do not heal simply because the knife has been withdrawn.

Post-communist Poland has not had to deal with the ethnic strife which continues to tear eastern and southern Europe apart today. Nazi extermination of Jews and shifts in Poland's borders after World War II, which had placed groups such as the Ukrainians back in Ukraine, had left Poland well over 90 percent ethnically Polish. This has been a central factor in its success in moving beyond communism.

One of Poland's main challenges today is to make the change from a dictatorship to a representative democracy. Though Solidarity was aptly named during the years leading up to the defeat of communism, once that victory was won, people splintered into a number of political groups. According to the authors of *Poland: A Country Study,* experts agree that "given Poland's strong sense of nationhood . . . the main obstacle to solving [its] problems [is] the acute fragmentation of its political system."[28]

After Lech Wałęsa was elected president in 1990, he was frustrated by the fact that it was not clear what the president's powers really were, or how to get government business done. Under the Communists, the party chief had some power, but generally decisions were not made without the approval of a committee of party leaders. There was a senate,

73

Lech Wałęsa was elected president of Poland in 1990.

but it was not freely elected and generally served only as a rubber stamp for party decisions. Now Wałęsa found himself the head of state in a country whose legislature was a mix of mostly small, warring political parties, all with passionate feelings about the future of Poland. Two issues about which people disagreed were how quickly industry should be turned over from the state to private owners, and the role of the Catholic Church in politics. Both these issues remain heated today.

THE LITTLE CONSTITUTION

To work through these issues it was first necessary to reach agreement on the roles of the president and the parliament. In fall 1992, the Little Constitution was ratified, so named because it was clear that it would be years before a full constitution could be agreed upon, and some things simply could not wait that long. The Little Constitution established that the president would be chief of state and the prime minister would be head of the government. As chief of state, the president was responsible for both the overall welfare and direction of the country, as well as representing the

LECH WAŁĘSA

Lech Wałęsa, the president of Poland between 1990 and 1995, was born in 1943 in a small village outside Toruń, in Pomerania. His family still farms there. As a child he dreamed of being an engineer, but his family was too poor and too uninfluential to be able to send him to college. He went to a trade school to learn to be an electrician and got a job at the Lenin shipyard in Gdańsk.

When strikes broke out around Christmas 1970 in the shipyard, Wałęsa was a minor leader, heading one column of protesting workers. The experience inspired him and from then on he became more deeply involved, giving speeches to workers and confronting management over workplace issues such as wages and working hours. Ten years later he emerged as the leader of Solidarity after another strike, and after another ten years he became president of Poland.

As president, Wałęsa found it difficult to hold together a group that had achieved its primary goal of establishing a democracy. He felt that both the Sejm and the prime minister had more real clout than he did.

Wałęsa's credibility as a hero was undercut in 1992 when accusations of involvement with the secret police during the communist era embroiled him and many of his closest ministers and advisers. Because many documents were destroyed or doctored, the truth of the accusations will probably never be fully known. However, it was common in those contentious days in Polish politics to try to discredit adversaries by hinting that they had been involved in illegal or immoral acts under communism, and it is likely that the reputations of many innocent people, possibly including Wałęsa, were unfairly tarnished.

Wałęsa lost a very close presidential election to Aleksander Kwaśniewski in 1995 and left office a somewhat bitter man. Despite his disappointment, Wałęsa will nevertheless be viewed as one of the great heroes of Polish history.

Lech Wałęsa, leader of the Solidarity movement.

Hanna Suchocka became the first prime minister of Poland in 1992.

country abroad. The day-to-day workings of the government became the prime minister's job.

The real core of the government became the prime minister's cabinet, whose appointees had to be approved by both the president and the Sejm. Under the Little Constitution, the cabinet had the power to make policy and laws without going to the Sejm; there were too many points of view in the Sejm to reach consensus quickly—or even at all—and the country could not wait while the Sejm argued. Overall, it was felt that this approach would work for Poland because it provided clear leadership but ensured those leaders had been chosen by a representative process. The system was given its first tryout in 1992 when Hanna Suchocka became the first prime minister of Poland under the Little Constitution with Wałęsa as the country's president.

TACKLING THE ECONOMY

In the years preceding the Little Constitution, people disagreed on how Poland would move from a communist economy, in which the state owns factories and all other means of production, to a capitalist one, in which almost all businesses are owned by individuals. Under capitalism consumers pay whatever it costs to make an item plus whatever profit is being charged. Wages paid are generally enough at least to buy necessities. Under communism, workers are not paid nearly as much, but the cost of food and other necessities is extremely low. The net effect is the same—people have enough money to buy what they need, but the communist economy had one major problem. For example, a loaf of bread might cost the equivalent of ten cents, although it really cost fifty cents to produce. The government would charge ten cents and simply swallow the rest of the cost. It had to do this because no worker in a communist economy could afford fifty-cent bread.

The government could do one of two things. It could continue to subsidize the real cost of essential things, or it could make sweeping changes such as eliminating price supports and hoping that the chaos and unhappiness would be short-lived while wages caught up with the higher costs of daily life. When the Polish government decided to try the second approach, the human cost was high. According to *Poland: A Country Study,* these "cold turkey" changes led to "a general feeling in Polish society that a market economy might not be worth the sacrifice needed to attain it."[29] Living conditions became so alarming that the government backed off on some of its policies, but life remained very hard and unsettled for Poles.

Today, Poles still have mixed feelings about the speed of change. Some feel that an initial period of hardship and challenge is unavoidable and simply needs to be endured. However, others feel that the sacrifices they have had to make are beyond enduring much longer. In a recent Associated Press article by reporter Monica Ścislowska, the differences of opinion about life today as opposed to under communism are revealed in the comments of two typical Poles. One says, "It is better now. Even when I had money, there was nothing in the shops. Now I have less money, but . . . if I have it, I can buy everything." The other says, "There were shortages of

THE BEER LOVERS' PARTY

With the fall of communism, Poles suddenly found themselves able to express their views freely and publicly. As a result many new political parties formed. Most of these parties were completely serious about their goals, but one exception was the Beer Lovers' Party, which registered as an official party in 1990. The Polska Partia Przyjaciól Piwa, or PPPP, started as a joke, having as its stated goal to promote open political discussion in taverns serving high-quality Polish beer. But much to its founders' surprise, the image of relaxed but lively debate struck a chord with Poles after decades of repression, and in the 1991 election the party won sixteen seats in the Sejm. In 1992 the party split into two factions, the Big Beer and the Little Beer Parties. The Big Beer Party changed its name to the Polish Economic Program in an attempt to gain more respectability. Without its oddball aura, it soon became just another of the small splinter groups which became part of Hanna Suchocka's coalition government in 1992, and both it and the Little Beer Party have since lost much of their original, surprising, political power.

everything—meat, toilet paper, shoes. Now shops are filled, but we have no money. I don't know what's better."[30]

The ten years between the fall of communism and today are obviously subject to many interpretations, and have been characterized by a mixed record of advances and setbacks. Though Poland has been seen by Western countries as the greatest success story in post-communist eastern Europe, many Poles are beginning to lose patience with the lack of improvement in their lives. Strikes and protests have become part of daily life. For example, in May 1999, farmers threatened to set up roadblocks nationwide to pressure the government to give more aid to farmers by, among other things, raising taxes, and thus prices, on imported grain and dairy products so that people would prefer to buy cheaper Polish goods. The roadblock campaign, the second in 1999, was called off when the government agreed to meet with the farmers to discuss their demands.

Another nationwide protest in 1999, this one by miners, was over layoffs of workers. Half the country's mines are scheduled to close over the next few years, and the overall work force in the mines is estimated to go down by sixty thousand. This would worsen what is already a serious unemployment problem in Poland. The government previously offered to give money equivalent to two years' pay to miners who quit mining altogether, and to find new jobs for those who did not. How the government can afford to make these payments and where they will find jobs for the other miners has yet to be seen. Furthermore, farmers and miners are only two of the groups calling for immediate improvements in their lives. Adding to the government's worries in mid-1999 was a strike threatened at a state arms factory, and a hunger strike by nurses, both caused by demands for higher wages in the face of inflation.

Poland's government is facing some unusual constraints as it tries to solve its economic problems. Workers' demands can usually be met one way or another by more money, but Poland would have to borrow the money. Banks such as the International Monetary Fund (IMF) are reluctant to lend the country any more money as it already has a serious budget deficit. Additionally, one of the Polish government's top priorities is being accepted into the European Union (EU), an economic partnership among western European countries which strengthens their economies through favorable trade arrangements, but it seems as if any help Poland gives its own people will push that goal further out of reach. To illustrate, earlier in the 1990s Prime Minister Jan Olszewski proposed increasing state spending on such things as welfare and agricultural subsidies, a proposal which would have helped many Poles meet their basic needs. His plan was never implemented because spending more money on welfare and subsidies would have cost Poland money it did not have. Simply printing more money would cause inflation; borrowing money would increase debt. Both high inflation and more debt would have displeased the IMF and set back Poland's efforts to become a partner in the European Union.

The European Union's requirement that Poland get better control of its economy before becoming a member has resulted in declining support by the Polish people for the idea of joining at all. By mid-1999 barely half of them approved of the goal of membership. Even those who still support the idea now see the target date of 2003 for acceptance into the EU as overly optimistic in light of Poland's continuing economic problems. But without membership in the EU, Poland is likely to remain poor and weak in relation to its neighbors for years to come.

ENVIRONMENTAL WOES

Joining the European Union has some other requirements indirectly related to the economy. For example, the EU requires industries of member countries to operate in a way which protects the environment. Poland is not even close to this goal. The communist government saw large factories spewing black clouds of smoke as a sign of modernization and disregarded the environmental impact of the waste they were putting in to the air, water, and soil. Poland's problem today is what to do about factories which pollute but also provide necessary jobs and materials. There is no easy answer because Poland cannot afford to make expensive repairs or build new factories. Poland would face "the prospect of severe economic disruption if they abruptly curtailed the industrial practices causing pollution."[31]

Smoke pours out of a factory in Warsaw. Most Poles feel that although pollution is a serious concern, it is a lower priority than their nation's economic problems.

Upper Silesia, among the most densely populated places on the continent, is said to have the worst atmospheric pollution in the world. Infant mortality, often used to represent overall quality of health in a population, is thirty deaths per thousand, five times higher than in western European countries. Water pollution is so bad all over Poland that 65 percent of the river water cannot be used for industry because it corrodes equipment. The Vistula River takes in so many pollutants along its course that it cannot be used even for agriculture. Statistics for 1990 show that 95 percent of Poland's water is too polluted to drink.

Obviously these problems affect the health of Poles and the overall productivity of the coun-

try. Yet it is difficult for the government to make changes because so many jobs are at stake. Most political parties still see preserving jobs as more important than cleaning up the environment, because that is the way voters see it. In a 1992 survey, although 66 percent of Poles said environmental problems were serious, only 1 percent said they were the most serious problem Poland faces. On the other hand, 72 percent reported economic problems were the most pressing concern.

Pope John Paul II waves to a huge crowd at a mass in Poland. Catholicism is not Poland's official state religion, but the church still exerts a strong influence over the government.

THE CHURCH IN CONTEMPORARY POLAND

In addition to the economy and the environment, Poland faces a number of social tensions as well. In many respects Poland has a stronger sense of cultural unity than many countries, due to its homogeneous population, but disagreements based on ethnicity, gender, and religion still surface.

The role of the Catholic Church remains a controversial one. Though more than 90 percent of the country is Catholic, there are deep divisions as to the role the church should play in the politics of Poland. During early discussions about the constitution, the church proposed making

POPE JOHN PAUL II

The church records in the town of Wadowice, twenty miles from Kraków, reveal that on June 20, 1920, a baby boy named Karol Wojtyla was brought in by his parents to be baptized. Within a few years both his mother and older brother were dead of scarlet fever. He and his father lived alone for much of Karol's childhood, but during the Nazi occupation of Poland, his father also died.

Wojtyla went to Kraków to attend the Jagiellonian University, but when his teachers were deported to concentration camps, he decided to leave school to pursue his education in a seminary. Wojtyla worked in a stone quarry during the days to earn a living, and eventually became a priest. He was first a teacher in a parish and then became an auxiliary bishop of Kraków in 1958. Within a few years he was named archbishop of Kraków, and then was made a cardinal, the second highest position in the Catholic Church.

When Pope John Paul I died suddenly after only a few months in office, the College of Cardinals had to hold a new election for pope. Although rumor had it that he was being considered, Cardinal Wojtyla was considered a long shot because in the five-hundred-year history of the papacy there had never been a non-Italian pope. When he was elected, he took the name of his predecessor and became Pope John Paul II.

John Paul II has now been pope for over twenty years. He is elderly and quite frail. In recent years he has made several trips to Poland to come closer to his native land and people—most recently in June 1999, a trip many feel will probably be his last. Pope John Paul II has been an extremely important symbol to the Polish people. He is remembered for his heroic stands against communism while archbishop of Kraków and for his unwavering message of religious tolerance, but he is probably most loved for serving as a symbol of Polish achievement and of the importance of the Catholic faith to the lives of Polish people.

Roman Catholicism the official state religion. The proposal failed, however, because opponents feared it would force Poles to follow Catholic teachings even if they disagreed with them. Though Catholicism is not the official state religion, it remains a powerful political force. Important government meetings are often opened not with a simple prayer of blessing, but with a full Catholic mass, showing that the church has maintained a stronghold on politics in post-communist Poland.

ANTI-SEMITISM

Many feel, however, that the church does not deserve its reputation as a moral presence in Poland today. Critics argue that the Catholic Church in Poland has been close to completely silent on the issue of religious and ethnic tolerance and does not do enough to find and punish anti-Semitic priests. The former chaplain to former president Lech Walęsa completed a one-year preaching ban in 1999 for announcing from his pulpit that Jews have no place in Poland's government, and that people should check the ethnicity of candidates in local elections and not vote for any Jews or Russians.

At the center of the issue of Polish anti-Semitism is Auschwitz itself. Although the vast majority of those who died in the Holocaust were Jewish, the Polish government has chosen to emphasize the other groups who died at Auschwitz as a way of sending the message that the camps should be remembered as a national tragedy, not just a Jewish one. Jews, however, feel that the government has gone overboard to make this point, at the expense of acknowledging the particular suffering of the Jews. An ongoing controversy surrounding efforts to recognize Christian victims of the Nazi death camps erupted in 1999 over the proposed removal of a large memorial cross installed on property bordering Auschwitz. A Catholic activist objected to the removal and instead encouraged people to bring more crosses to the property. Although the Catholic Church officially took a stand against the activist, and supported the removal of more than three hundred smaller crosses that had been left at the site, Jewish groups still feel that as long as the large cross remains, Poles are continuing to deny the Jewish focus of the Holocaust.

Their concerns may be difficult for outsiders to understand, but in Poland, where only approximately 10,000 Jews remain of a prewar Jewish population of 3.5 million, there are still occasional well-publicized claims that the Holocaust never happened. In 1999 prosecutors charged a university professor with violating a law banning public denials of the Holocaust in his recently published book. To many

"CHRISTIANIZING" AUSCHWITZ

In 1979 Pope John Paul II celebrated a mass at the death camp at Birkenau in memory of all those who had died there. The backdrop to the mass was a twenty-six-foot-high cross, which was later permanently installed on a lot bordering Auschwitz, near the infamous Death Wall, where thousands of prisoners had been shot. The idea of the cross was to serve as a reminder that non-Jews had died there as well, including a group of 152 Polish Catholics killed there in 1941. The cross was actually the second symbol of Christianity on the edges of Auschwitz. In 1984 a Carmelite convent was opened right against one of the walls of Auschwitz, in a building in which Nazis had stored Zyklon B poison gas.

The World Jewish Congress and many others were unsettled by these two events. Both cross and convent were perceived as attempts to treat Auschwitz as a marker of a significant event in Christian history. This might not have seemed so out of place if it were not for the fact that Poland has only reluctantly acknowledged that the Holocaust was directed at Jews. Mark Salter and Gordon McLachlan, in *Poland: The Rough Guide,* quote the 1947 decree establishing the site as a museum as saying that "a monument to the martyrdom of the Polish nation and of other nations is to be erected for all time to come." The emphasis on Poles was an affront to the Jews. It was made worse by the fact that Jews were not even considered to be Poles when the ghettos were erected, or when the cattle cars to Auschwitz were filled.

At Auschwitz, until recently, tourist pamphlets and museum exhibits treated Jews as just another of the victim groups. Auschwitz, to the communist point of view, should serve as a reminder of how the Poles had been saved from fascism, not as a reminder of the persecution of the Jews. Through persistence, Jewish groups have now forced some changes in this portrayal, but the nation still seems unwilling to acknowledge the fact that before anything else, Auschwitz was built to kill Jews.

Jews, there is little difference between denying the Holocaust happened at all, which is the professor's position, and downplaying that it targeted Jews, which has been the government's position. Thus, despite laws and the concentrated efforts by a few concerned leaders, anti-Semitism remains a factor in contemporary Polish life.

WOMEN IN POLAND

Being Jewish is difficult in Poland, but so is being female. Polish women today often feel that their needs and aspirations have been ignored in the post-communist era. Some feel that a major reason for this is the church's stress on their roles as wives and mothers. The church has taken a number of stands on other issues affecting women, such as its strong objection to abortion, but the church is only one factor influencing the lives of many Polish women. According to Solidarity activist and Amnesty International leader Malgorzata Tarasiewicz, "[w]ith the growth of unemployment, there are government plans to send women home from their jobs."[32] Women feel less supported on the job, as shown by vanishing support for day care centers. By 1992, more than half of the nation's day care centers, established by the communist regime, had been closed.

According to Tarasiewicz, "it seems to be generally accepted in Poland that a man needs a job more than a woman."[33] Surveys generally support this conclusion: Almost half of Poles—men and women, housewives and wage earners alike feel that women should not work outside the home.

Polish women at work in a vodka distillery. Female employees in Poland are often paid less than men, are given fewer hours, and are laid off first.

Husbands are not expected to do housework even if their wife is employed. This lack of help makes it even more difficult for a woman to find work because many companies do not want to hire people with so many outside drains on their time and energy.

In Poland no laws prohibit discrimination in the workplace on the basis of sex. Women are offered less money than male coworkers and given fewer hours when they do find jobs; they are usually laid off first. They tend to have unskilled, low-paying jobs and rarely manage to get the necessary training to advance. In a country already wracked by high unemployment, the relative disadvantage of women seeking employment has become disastrous.

Despite these obstacles, women in Poland still try to find paying jobs because the money is needed to support their families. Having a stimulating career, or greater social prestige, or money for luxuries, are rarely mentioned as reasons to work. Women generally do not perceive themselves, nor are they perceived by others, as important to the political life of the nation, or as leaders in any sphere. Hanna Suchocka, who served as prime minister from 1992 to 1993, is often pointed to as an example of opportunities for women in Poland, but she herself appointed no other women to positions in her government.

LIFE IN TODAY'S POLAND

Life in Poland is hard for most people. The country endures long, frozen winters, and in the summer, people swelter without air conditioning. Although in recent years food has become more abundant, and on festive occasions the Polish table is always piled high with a wide variety of special foods, on a daily basis Poles try to get by on simple, filling dishes like soups and bread, and on whatever seasonal foods they can grow or buy cheaply. Few people can afford cars, and public transportation, though inexpensive, often involves bone-rattling rides on crowded buses or streetcars. Poland has far fewer paved highways and roads in rural areas than the United States or western Europe, and thus travel between cities and towns is difficult. Most people live in small houses or apartments, frequently with members of their extended family, and have far less personal space or privacy than many Americans are used to.

Telephones and televisions are far more common than they used to be, but still rare. However, even in remote areas people find a way to watch television at least once in a while at a bar or café, or in someone else's home. Television has influenced many young people from the country to leave home for what they perceive as the excitement of the cities, and those who stay, according to writer Tomasz Parteka, "are often ashamed of the out-dated behaviour of their parents and grandparents."[34] Still, traditions run deep, and city dwellers tend to return to their hometowns for holidays; in increasing numbers they are setting up second homes in the countryside, which they visit on summer weekends to tend vegetable gardens and enjoy the peace and quiet.

Unfortunately, in both city and town, the hardships of life are often drowned in alcohol, usually vodka. According to Tomasz Parteka, "[v]odka flows like a stream through the average Polish village,"[35] and it would be a sign of poverty or

A view of picturesque buildings in Gdańsk, Poland's sixth-largest city. Most Polish city-dwellers live in apartment buildings, often with members of their extended families.

inhospitality not to provide enough vodka for any guest to get blind drunk. Under communism, alcoholism increased dramatically, and today it is a serious problem. Many people are killed in alcohol-related car and other accidents every year, and use of alcohol is also a factor in teen pregnancy. Because of the strong influence of the Catholic Church, according to Tomasz Parteka, "[t]here is no pity for the girl who gets pregnant before marriage, and she is invariably turned out of her home."[36] Poland's struggle to modernize clearly has created some social and family problems, as well as political ones, and it remains to be seen whether future generations can manage to hold on to the positive and minimize the negative aspects of their traditions.

POLAND'S CULTURAL HERITAGE

6

In Poland it seems that everything is splashed with color. In Kraków, sequins flash on the costumes of folk dancers. In the tiny town of Zalipie, the exteriors and interiors of houses, wagons, wells, fences—literally every surface—are covered with brightly colored flower paintings. In Zakopane glass is painted with bright designs. This desire to decorate is apparent inside churches as well, where statues and icons are often draped with lovingly sewn tiny clothes. Traditional decorative styles are centuries old, and reflect efforts to bring cheer into lives that are often difficult.

Folk music is upbeat as well, and so melodic that its dances found their way into classical music through Frédéric Chopin, Poland's best-known composer, in terms such as "polonaise," "mazurka," and "polka." Today, primarily in mountain villages in the south, the occasional fortunate visitor will be invited to a wedding or arrive on a holiday, and be treated to a nonstop festival of sights and sounds as brightly costumed dancers spin across the floor to tunes played by traditionally dressed small bands. Those not so fortunate are able to see similar performances by regional dance groups in folk festivals all over Poland and abroad.

These extravaganzas of sight and sound are testimony to the resilience of the Poles themselves—their sense of identity has survived two centuries' worth of attacks by foreign cultures. For example, when the Nazis invaded Poland, they destroyed two irreplaceable collections of early twentieth-century audio recordings of music performed in villages. After the war, under communism, collections began again, but the government only supported researching music that promoted the idea that peasant farmers were plump and

89

rosy-cheeked, and so happy with their lives that they could hardly resist bursting into song and dancing in the fields as they worked.

Despite such attempts to distort and destroy authentic Polish culture, it has survived. But traditional folk art, as distinguished from mass-produced souvenirs, is getting harder to find in modern Poland. This is due in part to the declining numbers of artisans practicing traditional arts, but also to the fact that many Poles today are less interested in their own folk culture than they are in Western styles of art and music. Polish youth may enjoy listening to traditional tunes for a little while, but will soon drift off to find a place to hear their

A GÓRALE WEDDING

In the foothills of the High Tatras in southeast Poland, the traditions of one of Poland's most colorful ethnic groups, the Górale, are still practiced today much as they have been for centuries. Górale wedding celebrations begin with the wedding party going to the church in horse-drawn carts, accompanied by another cart in which musicians play in the traditional Górale style, which consists of energetic sawing of violins and other stringed instruments accompanied by a unique style of high pitched singing. When the carts arrive at the church, the musicians serenade the bride and groom into the church, then follow behind to play music from the choir loft to accompany the service. After the ceremony, everyone goes to the largest hall in town, usually the fire station, and the music continues for most of the night. To avoid taking breaks, band members duck in and out individually to eat and rest during the course of the evening.

A typical Górale dance begins by a male guest deciding he wishes to dance with a particular woman. Rather than simply asking her, he goes up to the band and says a few sentences to them in a loud, declamatory (half-sung, half-spoken) style. The band then begins to play, and another man takes the chosen woman onto the dance floor. The first man dances a traditional dance alone while the second man dances a traditional dance with the woman. After a few minutes, the second man hands the woman over to the man who had asked to dance with her, and they continue the dance together. The overall dance thus becomes a little story that the audience finds very entertaining.

own music. Traditional floral designs may cover the walls of villages, but in cities, edgy posters abound.

LITERATURE

In the 1700s, the Polish Sejm ordered printers to donate a copy of every book they published to a national library. By the time the library was destroyed by the Russians at the start of the partitions in 1772, it had grown to half a million volumes. The massive size of the library shows the importance of literature to the Poles; its destruction shows what the Poles were up against, their literary heritage threatened as their nation was disappearing around them. But continue it did.

The village of Zalipe is famous for the colorful flowers and other intricate designs covering the clothing, bed linens, walls, and even the ceilings.

In fact, many argue that the golden age of Polish literature was only in its infancy at the beginning of the partitions. According to writer Ewa Malicka-Kingston,

> It was literature that kept Polish hearts uplifted during the many wars, gave them the hope and the strength to survive, provided examples of courage and steadfastness. During the partitions, when the Poles lost their independence, it helped to protect the national culture and language from outside interference. It was above all poetry that helped to keep alive Polish consciousness during periods of repression.[37]

The writer most associated with carving out this cultural role for Polish writers is the poet Adam Mickiewicz, after whom many streets, parks, and public places are named today. His romantic, impassioned verse in such works as *Pan Tadeusz* (1834) influenced generations of writers. Other important Polish poets are Julius Slowacki (1809–1849), Zygmunt Krasicki (1812–1859), and Cyprian Norwid (1821–1883). Unfortunately for non-Poles, their poetry is not easy to follow because it is steeped in references lost on outsiders. For this reason, these writers are not widely read elsewhere. However, many contemporary Polish poets have been able to reach wider audiences. The three most notable examples of the literary legacy of Mickiewicz in contemporary times are Zbigniew Herbert, Czeslaw Milosz, winner of the Nobel prize for literature in 1980, and Wislawa Szymborska, a poet who won the Nobel prize in 1996.

Novelists abound as well, beginning in the second half of the nineteenth century. Boleslaw Prus conveys life in nineteenth-century Warsaw in his 1890 novel *Lalka (The Doll)*. Henryk Sienkiewicz won the Nobel prize for literature for his novel *Quo Vadis* (1896) about life in ancient Rome. Wladyslaw Reymont also won the Nobel prize for *Chlopi (The Peasants)* in 1924. Fiction writer Tadeusz Borowski's collection of short stories based on his own experiences at Auschwitz, *Prosze Państwa do Gazu (This Way to the Gas)* won international acclaim; as did Jerzy Andrzejewski's 1948 novel *Popiól i Diament (Ashes and Diamonds)*, about a young man who kills another man whom he believes sold out Poland to the Communists.

THEATER AND FILM

Poland has been known for the last few decades for the unusual plays that have been produced on its stages. This is due in part to the Polish tendency to stress symbols and obscure references, but is also doubtless due to the repressive governments under which Polish dramatists lived and wrote. Polish plays are very visual, and props and sets often play as large a role in a production as the lines spoken by the actors. Prominent dramatist Jerzy Grotowski trained actors in mime and gymnastics, so they could convey much of the action without words at all. In some plays, particularly those of the modern Polish dramatist Tadeusz Kantor, animated props function as characters in the action. Grotowski and Kantor were very influential on playwrights around the world, who used their avant-garde ideas in their own works.

Perhaps slightly better known to international audiences are some Polish films. As with plays, according to authors Mark Salter and Gordon McLachlan, until the fall of communism, "the key issue for Polish film-makers used to be getting their works past the censors; for years they responded to the task of 'saying without saying,'"[38] by satire, symbols, and inside jokes that make many of their films a bit obscure. Roman Polanski is probably the best-known Polish filmmaker. He immigrated to the United States and became famous as the director of *Rosemary's Baby* and *Chinatown*.

Polish director Roman Polanski attended film school in Lódź and later immigrated to the United States.

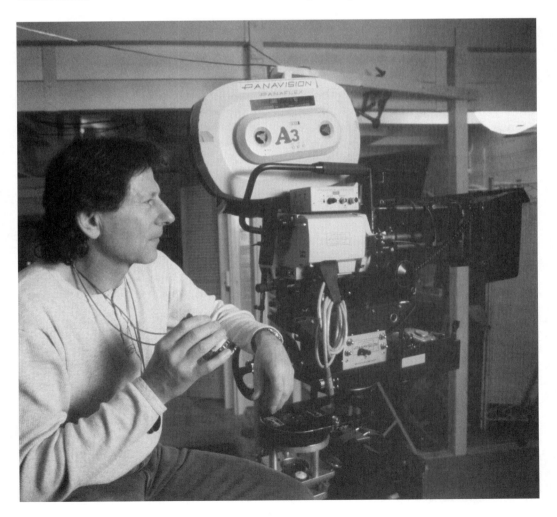

Polanski trained at the Lódź Film School, an internationally renowned institution functioning like a university for directors and camera persons. At Lódź, students take courses in literature and other subjects as well as in the technical aspects of filmmaking, so that they will be able to produce more literate, intelligent films. Also associated with Lódź is Andrzej Wajda, according to critic Jerzy Wojcik the "undisputed authority as far as young directors are concerned,"[39] and now a member of the Polish Sejm. His best known films are *Man of Iron,* about the Solidarity movement, which won the Grand Prize at the Cannes Film Festival in 1981; and *The Promised Land,* which was nominated for an Oscar for best foreign film in 1978.

VISUAL ARTS

Polish painting and other visual arts often make strong statements about how Poles feel about events in their country. Art critic Thomas Strauss points out that in the nineteenth century, "[a]s might be expected from a nation . . . divided against its will, [Polish art] dwelt in a world of hope and dreams rather than one of political and economic realities."[40] Polish painters such as Piotr Michalowski turned out huge paintings, boiling with action, of such Polish heroes as Tadeusz Kościuszko in battle, of Copernicus, dramatically posed as if on the verge of a great discovery, and beautiful landscapes showing the Polish countryside as a paradise. This was and continues to be a matter of no real significance to Poles. The important thing to them indeed was the specific subject matter because, during the partitions, painters such as Michalowski and Jan Matejko were keeping alive the history of their vanished nation.

By the end of the nineteenth century, however, one of the most important figures in Polish arts, Stanislaw Wyspiański, was taking art in a new direction which would bring Poland into the forefront of early twentieth-century modern art. Using the new ideas of psychologists such as Carl Jung, Wyspiański painted eerie canvases, both dreamlike and realistic at the same time, of his fantasies about medieval Poland, in which, according to Thomas Strauss, "all the demons of the country's past are translated into the alienated present."[41] Wyspiański's fame is not limited to such paintings: He wrote plays and other literature and was a well-known architect.

Since Wyspiański's time, artists have tended to focus either on their own private visions, or on abstract designs that barely, if at all, suggest any recognizable reality. A few artists made political statements about repression in Poland under communism, but for the most part, their criticisms tended to be veiled in symbols or framed as inside jokes. In the freer climate of Poland today, many painters make fun of their society, often portraying it as shallow, or focused on things that are not really very important. For example, one artist created a painting which was nothing but the Polish flag. It was controversial because it seemed to be treating the flag as just another object rather than as a sacred symbol of the nation. Today Polish painters, and painters of Polish origin living elsewhere, are highly respected and well represented in museums around the world.

CLASSICAL MUSIC

The development of music over the last two centuries has paralleled that of the other arts. In the nineteenth century exiled Polish composer and pianist Frédéric Chopin drew deliberately upon his ethnic roots to create original, distinctly Polish-sounding piano music, as did his less well known contemporary, Stanislaw Moniuszko. Later, in the early twentieth century, composers continued to weave Polish folk music into their compositions. The best known of these composers was Karol Szymanowski (1882–1947), who modeled himself after giants of his time such as Russian composer Igor Stravinsky, creating works in which ancient traditions and mythical stories are told in often jarring and disturbing melodies and rhythms.

After World War II, several major composers began creating works reflecting the feelings of devastation shared by many around the world. The titles of several of the best known of these pieces give some idea as to the somberness of their themes. Witold Lutoslawski was the first major postwar Polish composer, his most famous work being *Funeral Music*. A composer of even greater stature, Krzysztof Penderecki, followed Lutoslawski. Penderecki's best-known work is *Threnody for the Victims of Hiroshima*, written to commemorate the dropping of the atomic bomb on Japan by the United States at the end of World War II. In recent years Henryk Górecki has become internationally famous,

FRÉDÉRIC CHOPIN

Frédéric (Polish Fryderyk) Chopin was born in 1810 in a small village outside Warsaw. As a child he loved the folk dances he heard in the villages around his home, and throughout his career, he blended elements of Polish melodies and rhythms in many of his compositions.

Unlike other great composers, Chopin composed almost exclusively for one instrument—the piano, giving the world some of the most stirring and beautiful compositions for that instrument. He is known for the tremendous complexity of his compositions—in fact, few pianists are skilled enough to play some of them. According to Mark Salter and Gordon McLachlan in *Poland: The Rough Guide*, many Poles feel his music captures what it means to be Polish, "alternating wistful romanticism with storms of turbulent, restless protest—'guns hidden in flowerbeds,' in fellow composer Schumann's memorable description."

In 1838 Chopin met a wealthy woman who wrote novels under the pen name George Sand. Soon she became his mistress and benefactor, although she was much older than he. He went to live with her at her mansion in Nohant, outside Paris, and later in a villa in Majorca, off the coast of Spain. She used to spend hours at a time lying under the piano while he played, and claimed there was more inspiration and genius in a few seconds of his work than in many whole symphonies by other composers. In the nine years Chopin lived with Sand he produced the vast majority of his greatest compositions, including the *Polonaise Fantaisie*. In addition to being his mistress and most ardent fan, Sand was in many ways like a mother to Chopin, taking care of him after he contracted tuberculosis. Eventually they ended their relationship, and Chopin returned to Paris, where he died a little over a year later.

Today in Warsaw, concerts are frequently given under a large statue of Chopin, and his home is maintained as a museum.

particularly for his *Miserere*, written to commemorate the Solidarity members who died during the strikes which led the way to the fall of communism, and for his *Symphony of Sorrowful Songs*, which weaves a somber orchestral background and three soprano solos into a deeply moving composition.

HENRYK GÓRECKI'S THIRD SYMPHONY

Symphony No. 3 *(Symphony of Sorrowful Songs),* a beautiful and moving piece of music, was written by Henryk Górecki in 1976. The symphony has three movements. In the first movement the orchestra begins quietly and builds toward the introduction of a soprano, who sings a simple, achingly beautiful lament whose words date from the fifteenth century. The lament sings of a mother's love for her son, and ties her sorrow at his death to the sorrow of Mary at the death of Jesus.

In the second movement the soloist sings a wrenching melody using words found carved in the wall of a Gestapo holding cell in Zakopane, a town in the Polish High Tatra Mountains. The words are in the form of a prayer to Mary for help, but the somber tone of the singer conveys a farewell to life, because help is unlikely to come.

The soprano sings the words to a Polish folk song in the third movement, again a mother's lament over the death of a son. The orchestra's playing builds into a slowly pulsating, surging wave of sound, which flows into another melody, ending the symphony with words which music critic and Arte Nova liner note writer Stefan Lipka translates as, "And thou, God's sweet flowers, surround me in bloom, that my son may sleep peacefully."

The piece is written in what is commonly called minimalist style, meaning that the entire symphony is built with a limited range of notes and very simple, short melodic phrases. This gives the piece a meditative, hypnotic effect somewhat like Gregorian chant, but played by a large orchestra over which a simple, pure soprano voice soars. The symphony brought Górecki worldwide fame.

Composer Henryk Górecki has won acclaim not only in his native Poland, but internationally as well.

POPULAR MUSIC

Poland's popular music scene is vibrant, although few of its stars are well known outside Poland. The music divides into similar categories to those in the United States—from easy listening to punk, from new age to industrial, from folk music to good old fashioned rock and roll. On almost any night in Poland's cities, music is everywhere, from jazz clubs, coffee houses, and concert halls, to raves and punk nightclubs.

One of the few Polish singers to gain recognition outside Poland is Basia Trzetrzelewska, who records simply as Basia. Her style is best categorized as a fusion of jazz and pop, although her full repertoire is much broader, including renditions of Broadway hits. Her two best-known albums are *Time and Tide* and *London Warsaw New York.*

Apparently poised to reach a world market as successfully as Basia has done is the progressive rock group Ankh, which has been recording since 1994. Its style involves an unusual mix of instruments and vocals, including electric violins and viola, in addition to the more standard guitars and percussion. Another group mixing violas with vocals to create a unique sound is the group Sirrah, from the town of Opole in the heart of Silesia. In addition to Ankh and Sirrah on the easier listening end of the musical spectrum is Martyna Jakubowicz. She has recorded almost a dozen albums of what is described as folk-blues.

As different from Ankh, Sirrah, and Jakubowicz as could be imagined are the substantial number of heavy metal and punk bands who draw crowds of young listeners in the cities. Many have recorded albums but these recordings get little distribution outside Poland. Among the artists which have remained popular for more than a little while are: Sexbomba, a punk rock group; Fading Colors, Cryptic Tales, and Multicide, three heavy metal groups; and Liroy, a Polish rapper.

In a different vein from all of the previously mentioned groups are two bands who are finding a receptive audience for a style of music which fuses Polish folk music with other world styles. According to Roots World, an online site focused on international folk music, "There's not a whole lot of contact between Poland's new folk scene and the rest of the world, but over the years Poland has offered us some pretty interesting music,"[42] including what has now been a well-explored fusion of polka and reggae. One of the most energetic folk groups recording today is The Saint Nicholas Orchestra, affectionately called St. Nicks. Although some of their music would qualify as fusion, they are considered by the Roots World critics to be at their best when they are playing relatively straightforward Polish folk music, "pumped up to high-pressure by good musicianship and a generous love of the old music."[43] More daring in their style is the group Berklejdy. The central instrument is a cymbalom, or hammered zither. According to Roots World, in one of their recent pieces the sound "crawls out of the speakers with a raw, primitive wooden horn and then explodes into a slow, groove reggae number with a fat bass and drum kit, punctuated by electric guitar and accordion."[44] Other compositions by Berklejdy have Arabic, Indian, and other influences, all adding up to a joyful and unique form of musical expression.

One more artist to emerge recently in Poland is a Polish American who records under the name Leslaw with his trio, Partia. One of his parents is Polish and the other American, and Leslaw spent parts of his childhood in each country. He also split his college work between the two countries, getting a bachelor's degree from the University of Michigan and a master's degree from the University of Warsaw. But Leslaw's love is rockabilly music, and Partia, whose other two members are Polish nationals, plays a particularly energetic version in Polish, including a recent big hit called "Warszawa i Ja" (Warsaw and Me).

LEISURE ACTIVITIES

Culture, of course, consists of more than the arts. The Poles enjoy a wide range of leisure activities. Camping and hiking are extremely popular forms of recreation in the summer, and sports such as downhill and cross-country skiing and ice skating are equally popular in the winter. More daredevil sports such as rock climbing and hang gliding are also very popular.

Poles also excel at competitive sports. Polish Olympians did extremely well at the summer games in Atlanta in 1996, where they won seventeen medals, seven of them gold, including Renata Mauer's medal in the air rifle competition and Andrzej Wroński's in Greco-Roman wrestling. Probably the

Street musicians in Kraków play traditional Polish music. Folk music has endured in Poland and is often blended with foreign influences such as reggae and jazz.

best-known Polish Olympian is track star Irena Szewińska-Kirszenstein, who participated in five different Olympic Games and won three gold medals. Additionally, in her career she broke six world records and was the first woman in history to hold the 100-meter, 200-meter, and 400-meter record at the same time.

Even though Poland has produced many world class sports legends, many in Poland think of soccer first when they think of sports. Children especially love playing the game, and a few grow up to play on professional teams, including the World Cup team, although Polish teams have not generally been very competitive at the international level. Regardless of their limited success, Poles still come together as a nation to cheer on their team. Thus, from children playing on neighborhood teams to groups gathered around a television to watch the national team's progress in a World Cup match, sports are yet another way that the Poles come together to define themselves as a people. For good reason, most Poles feel that despite the hardships and setbacks they have faced over the years, it is a fine thing to be Polish.

FACTS ABOUT POLAND

GOVERNMENT

Official Name: Republic of Poland (Rzeczpospolita Polska)

Government type: Democracy

Administrative divisions: 49 provinces

Independence: November 11, 1918 (establishment of independent republic after partitions)

Executive branch: President Aleksander Kwaśniewski (1995); Prime Minister Jerzy Buzek (1997)

Legislative branch: Bicameral (two house) National Assembly; Sejm (460 seats established by proportional representation); Senat (100 seats, elected by province)

Elections: President, every five years, next in November 2000; National Assembly, every four years, next in September 2001

PEOPLE

Population (1998): 38,606,922

Population growth: –0.04 percent

Birth rate: 9.79 births per 1,000 population

Death rate: 9.76 deaths per 1,000 population

Infant mortality: 13.18 deaths per 1,000 live births

Life expectancy at birth: males, 68.6 years; females, 77.16 years

Ethnic groups: Polish, 97 percent; German, 1.3 percent; Ukrainian, 0.6 percent; Belarusian, 0.5 percent

Religions: Roman Catholic, 95 percent (75 percent practicing); other (Jewish, Eastern Orthodox, Protestant) 5 percent

Official Language: Polish

Literacy: 99 percent of Polish people over age fifteen can read and write.

GEOGRAPHY

Area: 195,427 square miles (312,683 sq km)

Capital city: Warsaw

Boundaries: Baltic Sea, Kaliningrad (Russian Federation), Lithuania, Belarus, Ukraine, Slovakia, Czech Republic, Germany

Terrain: mostly flat plain, mountains in southern border areas

Natural resources: coal, sulphur, copper, natural gas, silver, lead, salt

Land use: arable land, 48 percent; pastureland: 13 percent; forests, 29 percent; other, 10 percent

Major cities/estimated population (1995 figures):

Warsaw: 2,316,000

Lodz: 842,300

Kraków: 751,500

Wroclaw: 642,900

Poznań: 589,300

Gdańsk: 466,700

ECONOMY

Monetary unit: Polish zloty (Zl) (All the following monetary figures are in U.S. dollars.)

exchange rate: 3.54 Zl=1 US$ (January 1998 rate)

Gross domestic product (1997): $280.7 billion. Agriculture contributes 6.6 percent to the economy; industry—34.9 percent; services—58.5 percent. The growth rate is 6.9 percent.

Annual per capita income (1997): $7,250

Labor force: 17.7 million. Of these, 29.9 percent work in industry and construction; 26 percent in agriculture; and 44.1 percent in services.

Unemployment rate: 12 percent

Budget: revenues, $33.8 billion; expenditures, 35.5 billion

Industries: machine building, iron and steel, coal mining, chemicals, shipbuilding, food processing, glass, beverages, textiles

Agricultural products: grain (rye, wheat), potatoes, milk, cheese, fruits, vegetables, poultry, eggs, pork, beef

Exports: $26.4 billion. Main exports are intermediate manufactured goods, 38 percent; machinery and transport equipment, 23 percent; consumer goods, 21 percent; foodstuffs, 10 percent; and fuels, 7 percent.

Imports: $44.5 billion. Main imports are machinery and transport equipment, 32 percent; intermediate manufactured goods, 20 percent; chemicals, 15 percent; consumer goods, 9 percent; food, 9 percent; and fuels, 8 percent.

NOTES

INTRODUCTION: POLAND—PROUD AND FREE

1. Quoted in Thomas Urban, "A People at the Heart of Europe," *Insight Guide: Poland*. Singapore: APA Publications, 1998, p. 21.

2. Quoted in Monica Ścislowska, "Poland Marks '89 Vote Anniversary," June 4, 1999. AOL: Associated Press news service.

CHAPTER 1: POLAND AND ITS NEIGHBORS

3. Stanislaw Klos, "Through Little Poland," *Insight Guide: Poland*, p. 178.

CHAPTER 2: A NATION RISES AND VANISHES

4. Waldemar Paclawski and Alfred Horn, "A Glorious Past," *Insight Guide: Poland*, p. 30.

5. Mark Salter and Gordon McLachlan, *Poland: The Rough Guide*. London: Rough Guides, Ltd., 1997, p. 610.

6. Norman Davies, *Heart of Europe: A Short History of Poland*. Oxford: Oxford University Press, 1986, p. 303.

7. Paclawski and Horn, "A Glorious Past," *Insight Guide: Poland*, p. 33.

8. Davies, *Heart of Europe*, p. 306.

9. Paclawski and Horn, "A Glorious Past," *Insight Guide: Poland*, p. 36.

CHAPTER 3: THE STRUGGLE FOR SOVEREIGNTY: 1800–1918

10. Davies, *Heart of Europe*, p. 159.

11. Davies, *Heart of Europe*, p. 171.

12. Davies, *Heart of Europe*, p. 171.

13. Davies, *Heart of Europe*, p. 172.

14. Davies, *Heart of Europe*, p. 166.

15. Quoted in Davies, *Heart of Europe*, p. 161.

16. Davies, *Heart of Europe*, p. 163.

17. Davies, *Heart of Europe*, p. 183.

18. Davies, *Heart of Europe*, p. 184.

19. Salter and McLachlan, *Poland: The Rough Guide*, p. 614.

20. Davies, *Heart of Europe*, p. 238.

21. Salter and McLachlan, *Poland: The Rough Guide*, p. 614.

CHAPTER 4: BETWEEN TWO TYRANTS: POLAND UNDER THE NAZIS AND COMMUNISTS

22. Paclawski and Horn, "World War II and Its Consequences," *Insight Guide: Poland*, p. 47.

23. Israel Gutman, *Resistance: The Warsaw Ghetto Uprising*. Boston: Marriner Books, 1994, p. xxiii.

24. Quoted in Paclawski and Horn, "Rebirth: The Second Republic," *Insight Guide: Poland*, pp. 47–48.

25. Timothy Garton Ash, *The Polish Revolution: Solidarity*. New York: Charles Scribner's Sons, 1983, p. 31.

26. Paclawski and Horn, "The Communist State," *Insight Guide: Poland*, p. 60.

27. Salter and McLachlan, *Poland: The Rough Guide*, p. 621.

CHAPTER 5: AFTER COMMUNISM: POLAND TODAY

28. *Poland: A Country Study*. Washington, DC: Federal Research Division, Library of Congress, 1994, p. xxx.

29. *Poland: A Country Study*, p. xxxviii.

30. Quoted in Ścislowska, "Poland Marks '89 Vote Anniversary."

31. *Poland: A Country Study*, p. 62.

32. Malgorzata Tarasiewicz, "Women in Poland," *Poland: The Rough Guide*, p. 631.

33. Tarasiewicz, "Women in Poland," *Poland: The Rough Guide*, p. 631.

34. Tomasz Parteka, "A Journey Through Rural Poland," *Insight Guide: Poland*, p. 76.

35. Parteka, "A Journey Through Rural Poland," *Insight Guide: Poland*, p. 76.

36. Parteka, "A Journey Through Rural Poland," *Insight Guide: Poland*, p. 76.

CHAPTER 6: POLAND'S CULTURAL HERITAGE

37. Ewa Malicka-Kingston, "Literature," *Insight Guide: Poland*, p. 95.

38. Mark Salter and Gordon McLachlan, *Poland: The Rough Guide*, p. 51.

39. Jerzy Wojcik, "The Lódź Film School," *Insight Guide: Poland*, p. 107.

40. Thomas Strauss, "Art, Music, Theatre, and Film," *Insight Guide: Poland*, p. 101.

41. Strauss, "Art, Music, Theatre, and Film," *Insight Guide: Poland*, p. 103.

42. Roots World, "Poland on Roots World," June 13, 1999. www.rootsworld.com.

43. Roots World, "Poland on Roots World," June 13, 1999. www.rootsworld.com.

44. Roots World, "Poland on Roots World," June 13, 1999. www.rootsworld.com.

CHRONOLOGY

A.D. 375
Slavs begin settling in area now known as Poland.

966
Mieszko adopts Christianity, establishes a Polish state.

1025
Boleslaw I is recognized by the pope as the first king of Poland.

1138
Boleslaw III breaks up Poland among his four sons.

1226
Teutonic Knights are introduced into Poland.

1241
Tatars invade Poland.

1320
Kingdom of Poland is reestablished under Wladyslaw I.

1337–1370
Kazimierz III the Great rules as king of Poland.

1346
Discrimination against Jews is forbidden by ordinance.

1384
Jadwiga is chosen by nobles as Polish queen.

1385
Marriage of Jadwiga and Jagiello establishes joint kingdom of Poland and Lithuania.

1399
Jadwiga dies; Jagiello rules alone for forty-five more years, giving his name to the Jagiellonian dynasty.

1466
Teutonic Knights are crushed.

1500
Golden Age of the Polish-Lithuanian kingdom begins and lasts until 1600.

1572
The last Jagiellonian ruler, Zygmunt August dies; the Republic of the Nobles (elected monarchy) begins.

1717
This is the year of the Silent Sejm.

1772
Austria, Prussia, and Russia begin dismantling the nation at the first partition of Poland.

1791
Poles establish first modern constitution in Europe.

1792–1793
Prussia and Russia take more land at the second partition of Poland.

1794
Kościuszko's Uprising: a peasant force armed only with scythes routs the Russians at Raclawice.

1795
Third partition of Poland: Poland disappears from the map.

1807
The semi-independent Duchy of Warsaw is established by Napoléon.

1814–1815
The Congress of Vienna establishes the Congress Kingdom in central Poland.

1830–1864
Various revolts against the partitioning powers fail.

1872
Prussian ruler Otto von Bismarck begins the Kulturkampf.

1914–1918
Divided by the German, Russian, and Austrian empires, Poles fight against their compatriots in World War I.

1918
Independent nation of Poland is established; the Second Republic is declared.

1926
Józef Pilsudski becomes president in a military coup.

1939
Pilsudski dies. World War II is declared. Poland falls; General Sikorski establishes a government-in-exile in London.

1940
Labor camps begin receiving prisoners; Jews are ordered to ghettos.

1940–1941
The Soviet Union begins massive deportations and executions of Poles.

1941
The "Final Solution" is put in operation.

1944
Warsaw Uprising: Poles attempt to rise up against the Nazis and are defeated as the Soviets stand by.

1945
Red Army occupies eastern Poland; Yalta Conference is held.

1947
Communists rig election and establish communist rule in Poland.

1953
Joseph Stalin dies.

1956
Workers riot in Poznań; Gomulka is elected and promises liberalization of communist rule.

1970
Strike in Gdańsk results in use of lethal force.

1978
Karol Wojtyla becomes Pope John Paul II.

1980
Lenin shipyard strike in Gdańsk leads to the birth of the
Solidarity movement.

1981
General Wojciech Jaruzelski becomes party leader and de-
clares martial law. Solidarity is banned and its leaders are
imprisoned.

1983
Lech Wałęsa receives the Nobel Peace Prize.

1984
Father Jerzy Popieluszko is murdered by security police.

1989
Talks between government and Solidarity result in an
agreement to share power. Communists are resoundingly
defeated in a parliamentary election.

1990
Lech Wałęsa is elected president.

1992
Hanna Suchocka is appointed prime minister.

1997
Poland applies for membership in the EU and NATO. Jerzy
Buzek becomes prime minister.

1999
Pope John Paul II makes a two-week trip to Poland. Miners,
farmers, and others strike and show signs of unrest.

GLOSSARY

avant-garde: ahead of its time, usually used to describe experimental art forms

black market: trade in goods in violation of official regulations

collective: something (usually a farm) formed from many small holdings and operated as a single unit under state control

communism: system of government in which private property is abolished and in which goods (and the means to produce them, such as land, industries, etc.) are owned by the state, which makes them available to all as needed

deciduous: used to describe trees that shed and regrow leaves according to the seasons

deportation: forced removal from a country or region of someone considered an alien

despotism: dictatorial rule by someone with absolute power

entrepreneur: someone who sets up, runs, and assumes the risk of a business

ethnic cleansing: efforts to rid an area of a particular ethnic group

icon: religious image, usually small and painted on wood, used in religious devotions

imperialism: national practice or policy of expanding power by acquiring more territory or becoming politically influential in another country

republic: a form of government that has a head (often called a president) who is not a monarch

subsidy: gift of money by a government to a private entity to help it with something deemed helpful to the public

votive: referring to something offered as a sign of devotion or gratitude

SUGGESTIONS FOR FURTHER READING

BOOKS

Jay Heele, *Poland*. New York: Marshall Cavendish Corporation, 1994. A good review of Polish history and culture, this book has many interesting sidebars and good photographs.

Martin Hintz, *Poland*. New York: Childrens Press, 1998. This very basic text in an attractive format has been recently updated and republished.

Insight Guide: Poland. Singapore: APA Publications, 1998. One in an excellent series of guidebooks not specifically intended for tourists, this guide is full of information about culture, places, and history.

Gerda Weissman Klein, *All but My Life*. New York: Hill and Wang, 1957. Writing for young adults, a Polish Jew describes her life before the war and her experiences in Nazi work camps.

Christine Pfeiffer, *Poland: Land of Freedom Fighters*. Minneapolis: Dillon Press, 1991. This simple text focuses on historic figures and legends not covered in other texts.

WEBSITES

Inside Poland (www.insidepoland.com) This comprehensive site is full of information and links about general Polish news, culture, sports, business, city information, and history.

Poland (http://poland.pl) Although it contains excellent information and links, this site can sometimes frustrate the English reader (look for the British flag icon).

Polish Suburban News Online (www.polishnews.com) Published out of Chicago, this site includes good articles on Poland in addition to news about the Polish American community.

WORKS CONSULTED

BOOKS

Timothy Garton Ash, *The Polish Revolution: Solidarity.* New York: Charles Scribner's Sons, 1983. A thorough history of the early years of Solidarity through 1983.

Norman Davies, *Heart of Europe: A Short History of Poland.* Oxford: Oxford University Press, 1986. This excellent 450-page history complements Davies's two-volume classic history of Poland, *God's Playground.* Davies is an eminent Polish historian.

Israel Gutman, *Resistance: The Warsaw Ghetto Uprising.* Boston: Marriner Books, 1994. Published in association with the United States Holocaust Memorial Museum, this book gives an excellent and very readable discussion of the 1944 uprising, but sets it in the context of the wider society and times.

Israel Gutman, ed., *Anatomy of the Auschwitz Death Camp.* Bloomington: Indiana University Press, 1998. This is a collection of essays by a number of scholars on all aspects of the death camp at Auschwitz-Birkenau. Gutman, a survivor of three concentration camps, is a modern Jewish historian at Hebrew University and research director of Yad Vashem, Israel's national holocaust museum.

Celia S. Heller, *On the Edge of Destruction: Jews of Poland Between the Two Wars.* New York: Columbia University Press, 1977. Heller provides an excellent discussion of Jewish life and culture in Poland in the years before the Holocaust.

Bernard Jacobson, *A Polish Renaissance.* New York: Phaidon Press, 1995. These are biographies of post-communist era Polish composers such as Andrzej Panufik, Witold Lutoslawski, Krzysztof Penderecki, and Henryk Górecki.

117

Allen Paul, *Katyn: Stalin's Massacre and the Seeds of Polish Resistance.* Annapolis: United States Naval Academy, 1996. The author combines background information with interviews of survivors of Stalin's ethnic cleansing and dislocation.

Poland: A Country Study. Washington, DC: Federal Research Division, Library of Congress, 1994. This area handbook is filled with detailed information about all aspects of Poland's economy and population.

Mark Salter and Gordon McLachlan, *Poland: The Rough Guide.* London: Rough Guides, Ltd., 1997. An excellent volume in this series of travel guides, the book provides good sections on history and the arts.

Adam Zamoyski, *The Polish Way: A Thousand-Year History of the Poles and Their Culture.* New York: Hippocrene Books, 1993. This is a thorough, readable cultural history with good maps and photographs.

WEBSITES

Central Europe Online (www.centraleurope.com) This large news service provides up-to-date articles about all aspects of life in eastern Europe, including useful comparisons and contrasts of Poland with other neighboring countries. It contains links to the *Warsaw Voice,* with excellent articles infrequently updated.

Poland Factbook (www.cia.gov/cia/publications/factbook) The factbook site is an online edition of the U.S. government publication.

Roots World (www.rootsworld.com) This comprehensive website deals with ethnic music around the world.

INDEX

119

PICTURE CREDITS

Cover photo: ©1998 Ulf Sjostedt/FPG International LLC 1998
© Paul Almasy/Corbis, 7
Archive France/Archive Photos, 75
Archive Photos, 63, 69
© Bettmann/Corbis, 50
© Bernard and Catherine Desjeux/Corbis, 17
DPA/Archive Photos, 60
FPG International, 36, 57, 58
© Kenneth Garrett 1990/FPG International, 101
Giraudon/Art Resource, NY, 44
© Louis Goldman 1994/FPG International, 30
Bernard Gotfryd/Archive Photos, 14, 22
© Historical Picture Archive/Corbis, 27
© Hulton-Deutsch Collection/Corbis, 46, 51
Library of Congress, 38, 39, 53, 98
© James Marshall/Corbis, 85
© Michael Nicholson/Corbis, 92
© PA Enterprises 1983/FPG International, 91
PhotoDisc, 8, 16, 80, 87
Reuters/Kevin Lamarque/Archive Photos, 76
Reuters/Maciej Macierzynski/Archive Photos, 70
Reuters/Luciano Mellace/Archive Photos, 81
Ron Sachs/CNP/Archive Photos, 74
© Peter Turnley/Corbis, 94
© Earl Young 1991/FPG International, 32

ABOUT THE AUTHOR

Laurel Corona lives in Lake Arrowhead, California, and teaches English and Humanities at San Diego City College. She has a Master's Degree from the University of Chicago and a Ph.D. from the University of California at Davis.